Contemplating

GOD

the Holy Spirit

Contemplating
GOD
the Holy Spirit

A Devotional

LAWRENCE KIMBROUGH

B&H
BROADMAN
& HOLMAN
PUBLISHERS

NASHVILLE, TENNESSEE

Ten-digit ISBN: 0-8054-4085-2
Thirteen-digit ISBN: 978-0-8054-4085-0

Published by Broadman & Holman Publishers
Nashville, Tennessee

Dewey Decimal Classification: 231.3
Subject Heading: GOD \ HOLY SPIRIT \
DEVOTIONAL LITERATURE

All Scripture is taken from the Holman Christian
Standard Bible® Copyright © 1999, 2000, 2002, 2003
by Holman Bible Publishers. Used by permission.

1 2 3 4 5 6 7 8 9 10   10 09 08 07 06

CONTENTS

God is here.

True, there's a whole lot happening in that little statement. If heard above the worried whispers and sniffles in a surgical waiting room, this phrase is like a taut hug around the shoulders. If announced between songs at a church service, it's like a fine mist soaking our weather-worn faces in worship. If flashed across our mind in loud, red letters at a moment of sinful indulgence, it can jar the teeth loose from our perceived secrecy.

God is here.

Yes, the Son has returned to glory, where he sits in readiness at the Father's right hand, his work accomplished, awaiting the hour when his reign over all creation will be as visible as it is real.

And yet God is *here*. Right now. By his Spirit's indwelling presence, he is somehow nearer than the next second, more available to us than the air in this room, more imbedded into our being than the fingerprints etched into our skin.

We could easily have been left on earth to wait out our salvation, like plaintiffs biding our time for the settlement checks to arrive. But the God who is already there is powerful and compassionate enough to be here as well. Here with us. Here this minute. Here in Spirit.

What to Expect

These devotional moments on the Holy Spirit are yours to use in whatever fashion you desire. And although I'm sure you'll find your own way to make this book work best for you, I thought I'd give you just a few ideas.

Most days don't lend themselves to a lot of quiet time with God. But then again, there are *some* days—perhaps early Sunday mornings, or a quiet afternoon, or the night before your day off—when you could really invest some extra time into worship, prayer, and Bible reading.

I'm thinking this collection of expanded devotionals would be perfect for that, especially because they include a whole bunch of related Scriptures to look up. That'll give God's Word a lot of opportunity to soak in.

Or perhaps you're the leader of some kind of Bible study—perhaps a men's prayer group or a handful of families who get together at someone's house once a week or so. This book ought to be a nice fit for you, then, because it keeps you on theme for a fairly long period of time and doesn't leave you short on material after five minutes. It's not too much, not too little. Maybe it'd be just right for you.

But again, *you're* the one who knows best what you need. You're the one God has intrigued with the idea of discovering more about his Spirit, eager to know him better, to dive deeper than usual.

Let's see what he has to show us.

ONE

TO YOU, FROM DAD

Dads don't have to be great shoppers to know a good kids' gift when they see one. It really only takes about three ingredients:

You have to know what your children like. Some of them are crazy about anything with butterflies on it, or baseball, or blue to go with their eyes.

You have to know what they already have. If you're not sure which movies or video games they already own, you'll be going back to stand in the return line.

You also have to know what they need. The wrong gift can feed a bad habit or breed arguments at home over rights and privileges. Gift-giving does carry some responsibility.

But one thing's for sure: father-to-child gifts are far and away the most fun to give. And when your heavenly Father saw what you liked, saw what you had, and saw what you needed, he gave you his Spirit—to satisfy all three longings at the same time.

Father, thank you for noticing just what we needed and for sending us your Holy Spirit to ensure that we'd never have a need for anything.

"If you love Me, you will keep My commandments. And *I will ask the Father, and He will give you another Counselor* to be with you forever. He is the Spirit of truth. The world is unable to receive Him because it doesn't see Him or know Him. But you do know Him, because He remains with you and will be in you. I will not leave you as orphans; I am coming to you.". . .

Judas (not Iscariot) said to Him, "Lord, how is it You're going to reveal Yourself to us and not to the world?"

Jesus answered, "If anyone loves Me, he will keep My word. My Father will love him, and *We will come to him and make Our home with him.* The one who doesn't love Me will not keep My words. The word that you hear is not Mine but is from the Father who sent Me.

"I have spoken these things to you while I remain with you. But the Counselor, *the Holy Spirit— the Father will send Him in My name*—will teach you all things and remind you of everything I have told you."

The Holy Spirit is indeed a hard part of the Godhead to grasp. Though he's every bit as divinely eternal as the Father and Son, we tend to think of him as a New Testament invention, dormant until he made his famously fiery entrance at Pentecost.

But how much earlier than the second verse of the Bible does he have to appear before we get the message that he has always existed—before light and dark, before day and night, before trees and flowers, "hovering over the surface of the waters" (GEN. 1:2).

When the children of Israel were coming to flower in the early dawn of civilization, even then the Father had "put His Holy Spirit among the flock" (ISA. 63:11), shepherding them through grasslands and desert, through successes and failures, keeping his followers prospering and protected.

He was still walking among his people at the turn of a new era, somehow depositing a seed of deity into the womb of a young virgin girl, continuing to exhibit his presence in ways that had never ceased to amaze.

So we shouldn't restrict the Holy Spirit to our own stretch of history, as if we possess in him a share of God not available to millennia past. The Spirit has always been man's sense of the presence of God. He has always been on equal footing in the Trinity.

READ
PSALM 104:24–30

YOUNG AND OLD

And yet the arrival (if you want to call it that) of the Holy Spirit in Acts 2 did fulfill a profound aspect of God's eternal plan—to "pour out" his Spirit on us in a manner that would cement what Christ had accomplished on Earth. In so doing, the Spirit energized a rough-hewn band of followers—believers who knew that something life altering had happened to them through Jesus' death and resurrection but who needed an indwelling force of God-breathing power to bring unity and cohesion to their raw surge of passion.

Therefore, to the eager eyes of the first-century church, the Holy Spirit felt like nothing they had ever experienced before. He was the one their Lord and Master had told them of, the one Jesus had promised to speak to his Father about, the one who was to come upon Christ's return to glory and "to be with you forever" (JOHN 14:16).

And so, yes, though the Spirit is older than the musty dirt in your basement crawl space, he is younger and more alive than the folks who take their boats out on Sunday mornings and look for all the world as though they want for nothing.

He is the gift of God, just as the Son is, just as the Father himself is. Inside the incredible mystery that we do our best to explain as the Three-in-One, the Holy Spirit is God's eternal presence, sitting right here in our living room, making this wilderness walk of life something worth- while to keep tramping.

READ
JOHN 7:37-39

WINDOW TREATMENTS

But lest we get to thinking that this is all about us, like kids who wake up on Christmas morning with their want reflex kicked in high gear, we need to remember that God has his own reasons for giving his Spirit to us.

Again, to see this truth in action, our time line can stretch far back into Bible lore, imagining the sense of breathless amazement that rushed through Israel's eyes and heartbeats at the crossing of the Red Sea. As night fell on the numbing memory of this near- death deliverance, "the Spirit of the LORD gave them rest" in their hearts (ISA. 63:14), soothing them with the palpable touch of his presence.

Why, though, would God lead his people this way? Why not direct them to safety without the car chase, without having to run through columns of pent-up waves furious to return to their sea bed? Why must this gift of "rest" necessitate a flight of panic?

"You led Your people this way," the great prophet wrote, "to make a glorious name for Yourself" (v. 14). Rather than snatching us up to immediate safety, his objective in brooding over us with his securing, abiding Holy Spirit is to reveal his character to the world through his dealings with ordinary folks like us.

That's because you can tell a lot more about a father by see- ing how he treats his children than just by seeing what he buys for them.

READ
LUKE 11:11-13

6

DIG IN

One of the things that gave Jesus comfort in his dying hours (John 14) was knowing that his Spirit would always be here.

"I WILL ASK THE FATHER, AND HE WILL GIVE YOU ANOTHER COUNSELOR" (V. 15). All three members of the Trinity are present in this short statement. What do you learn about each?

....

....

....

....

....

"WE WILL COME TO HIM AND MAKE OUR HOME WITH HIM" (V. 23). What's hard about making yourself at home in an unfamiliar place? How is the Spirit able to do this in us?

....

....

....

....

....

"THE HOLY SPIRIT—THE FATHER WILL SEND HIM IN MY NAME" (V. 26). The Father has given the Spirit because the Son was obedient. How are all three active in your own salvation?

....

....

....

....

....

Experiencing God the Spirit Over and Over Again

1. **The Spirit is a gift from the Father.**
   One of the proofs the apostles gave to verify the reliability of Jesus' ministry was to point to the trustworthiness of the Father, who "has given all things" into Christ's hands and who "gives the Spirit without measure" (JOHN 3:34–35). Think of what the Father has continued to do in your life, consistently over time, to nurture and to rescue. He does it through his Spirit.

2. **The Spirit exposes and convicts us of sin.**

3. **The Spirit renews, restores, and refreshes.**

4. **The Spirit sets us apart for special service.**

5. **The Spirit indwells those who belong to him.**

6. **The Spirit gives us guidance and direction.**

7. **The Spirit empowers and emboldens us.**

8. **The Spirit gives us insight into God's plans.**

9. **The Spirit can be grieved and rebelled against.**

10. **The Spirit instructs us in the will of God.**

11. **The Spirit moves and repositions his people.**

12. **The Spirit unites the church in mission.**

13. **The Spirit fills us with joy and worship.**

14. **The Spirit endures with us to the end.**

Pray About

- A fresh awareness for who the Spirit is and what he does.
- The openness to trust him even when trusting is extra hard.
- Your deep love for the Father and his many blessings to you.

TWO

NOW YOU KNOW BETTER

Perhaps I shouldn't lead off so early in the book with this uncomfortable side of the Spirit's character—his surgical ability to expose our sins.

But I'm afraid that of all his attributes, I'm probably more familiar with this one than with any of the others. Heaven knows that he and I have been round and round on this subject many, many times, often not making it till lunchtime without sensing his familiar tapping on my shoulder.

But that's not the only good reason for placing this topic here in the first few pages. The Spirit's ability to diagnose and drain us of our sin almost always marks a beginning point in our lives. Repentance inevitably comes before revival. When the Spirit has dogged us the hardest, our best days in Christ are usually right around the corner.

So if peace and freedom can only be sprung from wells of brokenness, then I say we should quit complaining about the Spirit's hard line and embrace his rebuke like "the wounds of a friend" (PROV. 27:6). For that's what they are. That's who he is.

Holy Spirit, I could never cry enough tears to express my guilt and dismay. Thank you for mingling yours with mine.

I say then, walk by the Spirit and you will not carry out the desire of the flesh. For the flesh desires what is against the Spirit, and *the Spirit desires what is against the flesh;* these are opposed to each other, so that you don't do what you want. But if you are led by the Spirit, you are not under law.

Now the works of the flesh are obvious: sexual immorality, moral impurity, promiscuity, idolatry, sorcery, hatreds, strife, jealousy, outbursts of anger, selfish ambitions, dissensions, factions, envy, drunkenness, carousing, and anything similar, about which I tell you in advance—as I told you before—that *those who practice such things will not inherit the kingdom* of God.

But the fruit of the Spirit is love, joy, peace, patience, kindness, goodness, faith, gentleness, self-control. Against such things there is no law. Now those who belong to Christ Jesus have crucified the flesh with its passions and desires. *If we live by the Spirit, we must also follow the Spirit.* We must not become conceited, provoking one another, envying one another.

People are often fond of saying that God is more interested in making us holy than in making us happy. And, yeah, they're probably right—unless you take it to mean that he prefers it when we're *unhappy*, as if a good laugh should always be seen as suspect.

I mean, the Bible seems to teach that holiness and happiness are sort of hand in glove, like both ends of the same equation, joined at the equals sign. "How happy is the one whose transgression is forgiven . . . the man the LORD does not charge with sin, and in whose spirit is no deceit" (Ps. 32:1–2). Not only, therefore, are we able to be happy from a *salvation* perspective—happy that God has declared us "not guilty" in Christ—but also happy when sin *continues* to keep its distance from our hearts, when righteousness actually shows up in its place . . . like on a Thursday evening or something.

We tend to forget this a lot. We don't always put it together that when God said we could be happy by being holy, he meant that we could *only* be happy by being holy.

But the Spirit *never* forgets it. And as a result, all of us who bear Christ's name will routinely experience seasons of self-exposure when (as David said), "Day and night Your hand was heavy on me; my strength was drained as in the summer's heat" (Ps. 32:4).

There's nothing fun about this. His reprimand can make you feel worse than you've ever felt in your life. But David recognized what was happening here. Even through his own pain he could see the value of this, enough to beg God never to take his "Holy Spirit from me" (Ps. 51:11).

Because if God were ever to leave us soaking in our own sins, without showing us we'd jumped in the wrong stew pot, we and happiness would never be seen together on the same day.

READ
PSALM 32:1–11

LIVING UNDER ONE ROOF

We share a living room with the Spirit of God. He's right here. He never leaves. Wherever we haul these bodies of ours, whatever we pop in our mouths or let rattle around in our heads, God sees it from the inside out. When sin is still just a twinkle in our eye, before it's had a chance to work its way to the outside, the Holy Spirit has sensed it and felt it.

And it's not going to stay here.

In fact, when sin plops into our lives, when we let it lounge around and use the shower and drink our coffee, the Spirit makes sure we find out real quick that this is not good roommate material. The chemical reaction that occurs when evil tries sharing space with pure holiness is explosive indeed.

And that's the collision we're feeling when the Spirit throws our sin out on the doorstep. He hovers it right in front of our eyes where we can't miss it, can't work around it, can't enjoy a single thing without dealing with this clutter that's fogging up our spiritual windshield.

READ
1 CORINTHIANS
6:15–20

A NEW SPIN ON SIN

So this complimentary Holy Spirit rooter service that comes standard with salvation—itchy and agitating though it may be—is one of those cleverly disguised blessings God just gives us because we need it. It's like virus protection, like a termite contract. You wish you didn't need to have it, but you'd better be glad you do.

Besides, it's not like the Spirit considers his job done once he's completed his sweep and drawn red circles around our warning signs. His goal in our lives is not merely to convict us of sin but to lead us into righteousness, to help us see what we waste by keeping pride and bad attitudes on our payroll.

Sin is an opportunity cost. It steals from us the strength that comes from living in purity, the joy that flows from putting others before ourselves, the confidence that builds in us when Christ is not just relied on for rescue but enjoyed like a friend invited to dinner.

Only then can happiness occur.

READ
ACTS 2:37–40

DIG IN

Galatians 5 is not just a good place to find the fruits of the Spirit but also to find out what keeps them from growing.

"THE SPIRIT DESIRES WHAT IS AGAINST THE FLESH" (V. 17). Our flesh—the person we naturally are—is a scoundrel first-class. How well has life brought this truth home to you?

....
....
....
....
....

"THOSE WHO PRACTICE SUCH THINGS WILL NOT INHERIT THE KINGDOM" (V. 21). Saved sinners aren't kicked out of heaven, but what aspect of the kingdom do we lose by not loving it?

....
....
....
....
....

"IF WE LIVE BY THE SPIRIT, WE MUST ALSO FOLLOW THE SPIRIT" (V. 25). This makes such good sense, our only conclusion is to ask, "How can sin deceive us into believing otherwise?"

....
....
....
....
....

Experiencing God the Spirit Over and Over Again

1. THE SPIRIT IS A GIFT FROM THE FATHER.
2. THE SPIRIT EXPOSES AND CONVICTS US OF SIN.

   Sometimes the result of this purging makes us feel like we can't do anything right, as if we've messed up so bad that we'll never dig out from under the piles of regret stacked high on top of us. But the one who *exposes* is also the one who *disposes*. And if you'll give the Spirit room to clean house, you'll soon find your own body a lot better place to live in.
3. THE SPIRIT RENEWS, RESTORES, AND REFRESHES.
4. THE SPIRIT SETS US APART FOR SPECIAL SERVICE.
5. THE SPIRIT INDWELLS THOSE WHO BELONG TO HIM.
6. THE SPIRIT GIVES US GUIDANCE AND DIRECTION.
7. THE SPIRIT EMPOWERS AND EMBOLDENS US.
8. THE SPIRIT GIVES US INSIGHT INTO GOD'S PLANS.
9. THE SPIRIT CAN BE GRIEVED AND REBELLED AGAINST.
10. THE SPIRIT INSTRUCTS US IN THE WILL OF GOD.
11. THE SPIRIT MOVES AND REPOSITIONS HIS PEOPLE.
12. THE SPIRIT UNITES THE CHURCH IN MISSION.
13. THE SPIRIT FILLS US WITH JOY AND WORSHIP.
14. THE SPIRIT ENDURES WITH US TO THE END.

PRAY ABOUT

- Any resistance you've built against the Spirit's searchlight.
- Your refusal to let discouragement keep you down forever.
- God's gift of humility and how it would look on you.

THREE

BREATH OF FRESH AIR

I'm not going to say that Paul was in the habit of using bad language. But someone told me recently over a cup of coffee that in the Philippians 3 passage where (according to our new translations) he referred to his high-born, holy-boy heritage as "filth" or "rubbish," the King James Version might have been closer to his sentiment when it used the word "dung."

Or perhaps a word that means the same thing but that preachers don't say from the pulpit.

Again, I don't know. But even if Paul did hold back a little to keep from offending his readers' sensitivities —even if he didn't use a crude term to describe his pre-Damascus Road righteousness—it wouldn't have been untrue had he said it. Left to ourselves, without the benefit of God's Spirit in our lives, our best days really are rubbish. And even after we're saved, anything we try doing without him or against him is sure to stink to high heaven.

"The Spirit is the one who gives life," Jesus said. "The flesh doesn't help at all" (JOHN 6:63). So we'd better learn to let him take over.

Holy Spirit, all I do is mess things up. How I need your help, your refreshing, your encouragement.

Now if the ministry of death, chiseled in letters on stones, came with glory, so that the sons of Israel were not able to look directly at Moses' face because of the glory from his face—a fading [glory]—*how will the ministry of the Spirit not be more glorious?* For if the ministry of condemnation had glory, the ministry of righteousness overflows with even more glory. . . .

Therefore *having such a hope, we use great boldness*—not like Moses, who used to put a veil over his face so that the sons of Israel could not look at the end of what was fading away. But their minds were closed. For to this day, at the reading of the old covenant, the same veil remains; it is not lifted, because it is set aside [only] in Christ.

However, to this day, whenever Moses is read, a veil lies over their hearts, but *whenever a person turns to the Lord, the veil is removed.*

Now the Lord is the Spirit; and *where the Spirit of the Lord is, there is freedom.* We all, with unveiled faces, are reflecting the glory of the Lord and are being transformed into the same image from glory to glory; this is from the Lord who is the Spirit.

The Old Testament has some really great stuff in it. That "Daniel in the Lions' Den" story alone is enough to make you want to start praying three times a day in your kitchen. So just for a minute, let yourself be carried along down a stream of consciousness, remembering things like the burning bush, the morning manna, the boy Samuel hopping out of bed at night, King Solomon praying at the temple dedication.

Great stories. Good memories. God in action.

To see him loving a nation of quick-to-complainers, shepherding them through whole centuries of trauma and turmoil and their own hot and cold temperaments, the picture we get of his covenant with Israel is rich in both color and content. Queen Esther. Nehemiah on border patrol. The Twenty-Third Psalm.

But "if the ministry of condemnation had glory, the ministry of righteousness overflows with even more glory" (2 COR. 3:9). If you think Moses marching down the mountain with the tables of law under his arm is impressive (you've seen Charlton Heston), then try to imagine what God is accomplishing in our world this very minute and see if it's not also epic in nature.

Medical missionaries treating AIDS patients in Africa. Accomplished musicians playing to huge crowds and giving God every note of praise. Soldiers conducting Bible studies in Islam's backyard. Prayer partners holding hands and wiping away tears around a suburban dining room table. Great and small. Grand and in miniature.

The Spirit is making this thing more special by the moment.

> READ
> ROMANS 7:4–6

LIFE FOR THE TAKING

Because of the Holy Spirit, we are still today living in biblical times and able to experience God at work all around us—renewing us, restoring us, rejuvenating us.

Because of him, we have hope. I don't care what you're dealing with right now, how searing the pain, how black the prognosis. God's Holy Spirit is alive in you and prepared to be your full day's supply.

Because of him, we have life. We don't have to count up how much praying we've done this month, hoping it's been enough to satisfy God's appetite. We don't have to wonder if that one extra biscuit we ate for breakfast has irritated him into silence. We don't have to perform our disciplines as if we're taking medicine, every hour on the hour, concerned that one little bobble might bring on his wrath.

Because of him, we have freedom. And just because this liberty remains subject to abuse—with all the selfishness and deceit still floating around inside us—this doesn't mean we should be wary about embracing it. That's what the Spirit came for—to turn us loose, to set us free, to unhinge us from having to make grades and keep score.

Actually, this freedom was always available to God's people. His desire was never to set up a department for sacrifice enforcement. "If I were hungry, I would not tell you," he said to those who worshipped him by ounces and measuring spoons. "Sacrifice a thank offering to God, and pay your vows to the Most High" (PS. 50:12, 14)—not because you *must* but because you can.

So let's ask ourselves—we who live this side of the cross, who have the Spirit poured out on us in full measure—are we living in his freedom today? Are we walking in his hope? Are we accessing the life he's bursting to give us?

READ
ROMANS 5:1–5

ZOOM, ZOOM

We can. Jesus did.

When he offered himself to the Father, freely releasing his rights and privileges for a grander purpose, he found his courage "through the eternal Spirit" (HEB. 9:14). When he busted back through the thorny hedgerows of death, leading a train of captives from bondage to blessing, he did it "according to the Spirit of holiness" (ROM. 1:4).

And that selfsame Spirit is planted deep inside you today, a dynamo with enough energy and enthusiasm swirling inside to make a NASCAR race look like grandmas in Scooter chairs.

If you've been down in the dumps lately, you can stay there if

READ
ISAIAH 32:14–18

you want to. But you don't have to because renewal and refreshment are less than a whisper away.

DIG IN

"Where the Spirit of the Lord is, there is freedom" (v. 17) and a whole lot more, according to 2 Corinthians 3.

"HOW WILL THE MINISTRY OF THE SPIRIT NOT BE EVEN MORE GLORIOUS?" (v. 8). Think of what we now possess by means of the Spirit of Christ. Why is this not always interesting to us?

....

....

....

....

....

"HAVING SUCH A HOPE, WE USE GREAT BOLDNESS" (v. 12). Hope. Boldness. In what ways do you see these traits active in those believers whom you most look up to and admire?

....

....

....

....

....

"WHENEVER A PERSON TURNS TO THE LORD, THE VEIL IS REMOVED" (v. 16). Do you see "the veil" at work in today's world? In what ways do you sense it still impinging on your own life?

....

....

....

....

....

Experiencing God the Spirit Over and Over Again

1. The Spirit is a gift from the Father.

2. The Spirit exposes and convicts us of sin.

3. The Spirit renews, restores, and refreshes.
   Before we can experience the Spirit's ongoing newness, we need to remember just how rotten and stale our oldness really is. But armed with such emptiness, we believers in Christ are in the best shape of our lives to be encouraged, optimistic, and fully at rest with what the Spirit is doing in us. It's a freshness you can feel from toenail to fingertip.

4. The Spirit sets us apart for special service.

5. The Spirit indwells those who belong to him.

6. The Spirit gives us guidance and direction.

7. The Spirit empowers and emboldens us.

8. The Spirit gives us insight into God's plans.

9. The Spirit can be grieved and rebelled against.

10. The Spirit instructs us in the will of God.

11. The Spirit moves and repositions his people.

12. The Spirit unites the church in mission.

13. The Spirit fills us with joy and worship.

14. The Spirit endures with us to the end.

Pray About

- The discernment to see the holes in unspiritual living.
- Situations in your life that are ready-made for renewal.
- The privilege of sharing the Spirit's strength with others.

FOUR

FOR HIM ALONE

Sometimes in life our greatest blessings bear a close relation to our greatest fears.

The achievement of a happy marriage, for example, may mean having to confess an embarrassing habit we'd been able to keep to ourselves all these years. Having a baby compresses into one day more painful breathing and prodding doctors than some people endure in a lifetime. Graduating from college in a certain degree program may require that we take at least one class from a man known only as the Time Bandit.

In similar fashion one of the most powerful components of our relationship with Christ incorporates a fear most of us bring with us from about the fifth grade on—the fear of being tapped for an assignment far above our skill level, being given a special task we're not sure we can accomplish, being made to feel different, vulnerable, or exposed.

But when the Holy Spirit sets us apart for himself, when he gives us a job that alarms us with its scope, sacrifice, and complexity, he's really inviting us to experience the nearness to him we've always wanted. In the midst of fear . . . ultimate fulfillment.

Spirit of God, sometimes you scare me, but always you love me. I can't do all you ask, but I know you can do it in me.

The Spirit of the Lord GOD is on Me, because the LORD has anointed Me to bring good news to the poor. *He has sent Me to heal the brokenhearted, to proclaim liberty to the captives, and freedom* to the prisoners; to proclaim the year of the LORD's favor, and the day of our God's vengeance; to comfort all who mourn, to provide for those who mourn in Zion; to give them a crown of beauty instead of ashes, festive oil instead of mourning, and splendid clothes instead of despair. And they will be called righteous trees, planted by the LORD, to glorify Him.

They will rebuild the ancient ruins; they will restore the former devastations; they will renew the ruined cities, the devastations of many generations. Strangers will stand and feed your flocks, and foreigners will be your plowmen and vinedressers. But *you will be called the LORD's priests;* they will speak to you as *ministers of our God;* you will eat the wealth of the nations, and you will boast in your riches. . . .

Their descendants will be known among the nations, and their prosperity among the peoples. *All who see them will recognize that they are a people the LORD has blessed.*

Try putting yourself in this scene. It's nighttime, the third evening since Jesus has been dead. There hasn't been much sleep in the last few days. About an hour at a time, maybe. No more than two. Even then, every creak and rustle has been magnified out of measure. If Christ's apostles had ever felt on top of the world, this is how it must have felt to be completely underneath it. The pressure. The panic. The pulsing, racing heartbeat that pounds in your palms, your temples, your eye sockets.

All eleven of you are still there in one room. All but the one whose eerie absence casts an even darker pall on this whole situation. And everyone has reverted to their own basic survival mode.

Some have sat quietly, brooding, thinking. Others have nervously jumped from one mood to the next—sometimes looking frantic, sometimes fatigued, always fidgety. The doors are locked, mostly to keep people out but partly because you don't know where you'd go if the doors were open.

Then suddenly—Jesus is there! Not just a presence but a person. He uncurls his hands, revealing real lacerations, right where the nails had sliced through. He pulls back his robe, pointing to a clean wound the identical size of a spear blade.

Then in holy silence he closes his eyes, lifts his hands, purses his lips, blows a warm, steady breath into the air, and says, "Receive the Holy Spirit" (JOHN 20:22).

Knees nearly buckle. There's a tingling on each arm, vibrating through every pore of skin. This is power. This is riveting! (Blink your eyes. Swallow hard.) And it's real!

READ
JOHN 3:5–8

MEN ON A MISSION

We may not be able to feel it just the way the Eleven did in that electric moment, face-to-face with Jesus, dealing with both the immediate shock of his resurrected presence and the rush of his Spirit at the same time.

But in every bit the same manner, we who have trusted in the risen Christ have been commissioned and sealed with his Spirit, just as the first apostles were. We have been set apart—"consecrated," to use a good Bible word—chosen for holy purposes and placed in the Spirit's safekeeping.

That's not to say that "safe" is always a fitting description for how it feels to be stamped with his approval and blessing. When the Spirit said to the leaders of the Antioch church, "Set apart for Me Barnabas and Saul for the work that I have called them to" (ACTS 13:2), that work involved things like being pummeled with rocks, dragged out of the city, and left for dead.

Yet the Spirit continued to inspire and sustain them, pulling them up off the deck and back into duty, enabling them joyfully

READ
ACTS 20:28–32

to proclaim the gospel . . . like people who had truly and finally learned what life was all about.

GOOD AND READY

So if self-esteem is something that's always come hard for you, let this spiritual birthright feel like the honor it is—a placement of value, not on what you do or how you look or where you live but on who you are. The Holy Spirit has crowned your head with eternal blessing and approval. He has set you apart and counted you among his favored ones.

Likewise, if risk and unease is something you avoid like the measles, try coming to grips with the fact that this life is pretty much nothing *but* risk and unease . . . for everybody! But those who've been sanctified by the Spirit of God are no longer bound by the confining limits of eighty years and a nest egg. In him we have been given forever—already!—complete with all the privileges and peace dividends that come with eternal security.

It won't be easy. It won't be ice cream. It won't be "a place for everything, and everything in its place." It won't always fit on its own designated line in your DayTimer.

But it *will* be your earthly taste of purpose and destiny, your experience of true calling and meaning. The Spirit's blessing will be worth every peril and will take you where you really want to be.

READ
EZEKIEL 2:1–7

DIG IN

It's not a total stretch to read the Messiah's prophecy in Isaiah 61 and see a little bit of ourselves in there, as well.

"HE HAS SENT ME TO HEAL THE BROKENHEARTED, TO PROCLAIM LIBERTY . . . AND FREEDOM" (V. 1). The Spirit will always task us with weighty assignments. What are some he's given you?

....

....

....

....

....

"YOU WILL BE CALLED THE LORD'S PRIESTS; . . . MINISTERS OF OUR GOD" (V. 6). In what ways does the Spirit call us to live out this mission? Why is ministry an obligation for all of us?

....

....

....

....

....

"ALL WHO SEE THEM WILL RECOGNIZE THAT THEY ARE A PEOPLE THE LORD HAS BLESSED" (V. 9). How do you "recognize" the Lord's blessing on others? How do they spot it in you?

....

....

....

....

....

Experiencing God the Spirit Over and Over Again

1. The Spirit is a gift from the Father.
2. The Spirit exposes and convicts us of sin.
3. The Spirit renews, restores, and refreshes.
4. The Spirit sets us apart for special service.

   If this were all about talent, the plan of salvation would have come with an audition and an application procedure. If it were all about smarts, it would've been worked up as a standardized test with all kinds of qualifying percentiles for acceptance. But actually it's all about the Spirit, who not only calls us into his service but also gives us everything we need to carry it out.

5. The Spirit indwells those who belong to him.
6. The Spirit gives us guidance and direction.
7. The Spirit empowers and emboldens us.
8. The Spirit gives us insight into God's plans.
9. The Spirit can be grieved and rebelled against.
10. The Spirit instructs us in the will of God.
11. The Spirit moves and repositions his people.
12. The Spirit unites the church in mission.
13. The Spirit fills us with joy and worship.
14. The Spirit endures with us to the end.

Pray About

- The grace to see yourself through his eyes, not your own.
- Your willingness to pursue his will at all costs and hazards.
- A desire for eternity in your thoughts, motives, and appetites.

FIVE
AN INSIDE JOB

I t's a good thing the Holy Spirit didn't decide it was enough just to live in the same house with us or watch over us from the outside because our outsides can rarely be trusted to give accurate readings.

It's not all that uncommon, for instance, for a flat stomach to disguise a dangerously high cholesterol level or a blockage in one artery. A smart outfit and a matching smile can sometimes mask a deeply hidden fear of failure or a home life that's falling apart faster than anyone else could possibly guess.

Outsides lie. Not always, not invariably. But they do lie. A lot.

That's why the Spirit knew we needed him on the *inside*, way down low where secret thoughts and insecurities can grow sharp, gouging edges that tear up the landscape and carve deep grooves in our character. If he didn't go to work underneath, where the truth is exposed, where the circuit breakers are housed, where our spiritual infrastructure is being formed and fashioned, he'd be constantly diagnosing symptoms but not meeting our real needs.

Yes, it's a good thing the Spirit is in and still making house calls.

Holy Spirit, you are welcome here, not to leave me as I am, but to change me from the inside out.

I will take you from the nations and gather you from all the countries, and will bring you into your own land. I will also sprinkle clean water on you, and you will be clean. I will cleanse you from all your impurities and all your idols. I will give you a new heart and put a new spirit within you; I will remove your heart of stone and give you a heart of flesh. *I will place My Spirit within you and cause you to follow My statutes* and carefully observe My ordinances. Then you will live in the land that I gave your fathers; you will be My people, and I will be your God. *I will save you from all your uncleanness.* I will summon the grain and make it plentiful, and will not bring famine on you. I will also make the fruit of the trees and the produce of the field plentiful, so that you will no longer experience reproach among the nations on account of famine.

Then they will say: *This land that was desolate has become like the garden of Eden.* The cities that were once ruined, desolate, and destroyed are [now] fortified and inhabited. Then the nations that remain around you will know that I, the LORD, have rebuilt what was destroyed and have replanted what was desolate.

One of the most interesting things I'm discovering in writing this little book (we've talked about this before) is how present and evident the Holy Spirit is from one end of the Bible to the other. This is a clear indication that God, who has always known just how desperately we need him, has likewise always loved us enough to be here and help us out.

Even the Egyptian pharaoh noticed the difference in Joseph, a man who had "the spirit of God in him" (GEN. 41:38). It was God's Spirit that also filled the early craftsmen who fashioned the sacred implements of Israel's worship (EXOD. 31:3). "The Spirit of the LORD" rested as well on the great judges and warrior deliverers of the Jewish people, such as Othniel and Gideon (JUDG. 3:10 and 6:34).

John the Baptist was "filled with the Holy Spirit while still in his mother's womb" (LUKE 1:15). Peter was infused with Spirit power every time he stood up to open his mouth, it seems, during the exciting first days of the early church (ACTS 4:8). And when Ananias, the humble disciple from Damascus, laid his hands on a still blind and shell-shocked Christian killer named Saul, this budding missionary giant was "filled with the Holy Spirit" until the "scales fell from his eyes" (ACTS 9:17–18).

He's everywhere you look—the Holy Spirit, indwelling his people with the power they need to transform their lives and serve in honor of his name.

READ
ACTS 11:22–24

MIXED SIGNALS

But there's an alarming mention of the Holy Spirit in one of the more tragic events from the Old Testament. "The Spirit of the LORD" once enveloped the life of a fighting man named Jephthah while he was in hot pursuit of Israel's enemies (JUDG. 11:29). But strangely, Jephthah's initial reaction to this influx of energy was to inflate his own pride, cloaking his personal ambitions in a thick gauze of spiritual horn-honking.

Sort of like when we throw the weight of God into a discussion, figuring it'll make people more likely to go along with what we want.

But the promise Jephthah had made to the Lord—to sacrifice as a burnt offering the first thing to walk out the door of his house when he returned home in victory—became intensely personal when his only child, his precious daughter, rushed out to greet him, tambourines jingling. Then to add insanity to his stupidity, he *went through* with his vow—as if God would rather see him keep a cocky promise than choose life over death.

This is a grim object lesson to teach us that we can sometimes abuse the indwelling Holy Spirit, deceiving ourselves into believing that any sort of spiritual thought which pops into our head must of necessity be from God. Truth is, until the day we die, we'll always be subject to mingling some measure of self along with the Spirit's guidance. And while daily trust and obedience does keep it easier to tell the two apart, it's still never easy.

If the Spirit is really to have his way with us, it's not enough for

READ
GALATIANS 3:1–5

him just to be there. He needs to have every ounce of us under his control . . . more each day, more each moment.

COMES WITH A FREE GIFT

That's when the various gifts of the Spirit, given to each of us "according to [God's] grace" (ROM. 12:6), are fully released to flow through us like waves down a water slide. As our surrender becomes more and more complete, as his square footage becomes more and more spacious in us—that's when serving, teaching, exhorting, giving, and all those mighty and merciful ministries he's imparted to us will take on their true effervescence.

Because, yes, he's in there. But he also wants to come out through our hearts and lives and everyday activity.

Every one of us longs to be truly Spirit filled, not just merely housing his presence but making him feel at home. This has been the passion of God's people for a long time. I sure do want it to be mine. Don't you?

READ
HEBREWS 2:1–4

DIG IN

Ezekiel made a promise to God's people (chapter 36) that the Spirit would make all things new for them.

"I WILL PLACE MY SPIRIT WITHIN YOU AND CAUSE YOU TO FOLLOW MY STATUTES" (V. 27). Why is there such a connection between the Spirit's indwelling and our own obedience?

....
....
....
....
....

"I WILL SAVE YOU FROM ALL YOUR UNCLEANNESS" (V. 29). How have you experienced the Spirit dealing with you in these areas—purity of heart, purity of thought, purity of motives?

....
....
....
....
....

"THIS LAND THAT WAS DESOLATE HAS BECOME LIKE THE GARDEN OF EDEN" (V. 35). How much of God's sheer delight do we truly expect to experience in this life? Why or why not?

....
....
....
....
....

Experiencing God the Spirit Over and Over Again

1. The Spirit is a gift from the Father.
2. The Spirit exposes and convicts us of sin.
3. The Spirit renews, restores, and refreshes.
4. The Spirit sets us apart for special service.
5. The Spirit indwells those who belong to him.
   If it's unnerving to know that pure holiness resides within you, shedding stark light on the dusty corners and baseboards of your heart, try looking at it this way. Let it instead be a true relief that this one who dwells inside you is a full-service cleaning crew, creator, manufacturer, and makeover specialist. He can do a lot better job at this than you ever could.
6. The Spirit gives us guidance and direction.
7. The Spirit empowers and emboldens us.
8. The Spirit gives us insight into God's plans.
9. The Spirit can be grieved and rebelled against.
10. The Spirit instructs us in the will of God.
11. The Spirit moves and repositions his people.
12. The Spirit unites the church in mission.
13. The Spirit fills us with joy and worship.
14. The Spirit endures with us to the end.

Pray About

- What it really means to be a sanctuary of the Holy Spirit.
- Ways you've rebelled against his under-the-skin presence.
- Wanting him to reveal to you better ways to serve him.

SIX

SOMEONE TO GUIDE ME

For those of us who aren't too handy around the house, it would be so great to know of one person we could call anytime anything went wrong with an appliance, a computer, or a water pipe.

Sure, just about all of us have friends who can give advice and solutions on one area of expertise or another, like electronics or car engines or refinishing furniture. But when something springs a leak, jams in the printer, or happens in the fuse box, often our only option is just to flip a coin on the Yellow Pages and make plans to be home between 9:00 and 3:00 next Tuesday.

But we might be able to avoid it—the repair call and the $50 service charge—if we just had somebody who could diagnose the problem for us, tell us what part to go buy, or let us know if it's something we could put off for a while without hurting anything.

Thankfully, when it comes to the really significant issues and decisions of life, we do have such a Person. The wise, wonderful, and indwelling Holy Spirit is our faithful guide through all things. Let's see what he says to do.

Holy Spirit, it's not always easy to know where you're leading, but help me always to know that I can trust you.

There was a man in Jerusalem whose name was Simeon. *This man was righteous and devout,* looking forward to Israel's consolation, *and the Holy Spirit was on him.* It had been revealed to him by the Holy Spirit that he would not see death before he saw the Lord's Messiah. *Guided by the Spirit, he entered the temple complex.* When the parents brought in the child Jesus to perform for Him what was customary under the law, Simeon took Him up in his arms, praised God, and said:

"Now, Master, You can dismiss Your slave in peace, according to Your word. For my eyes have seen Your salvation. You have prepared [it] in the presence of all peoples—a light for revelation to the Gentiles and glory to Your people Israel."

His father and mother were amazed at what was being said about Him. Then Simeon blessed them and told his mother Mary: "Indeed, this child is destined to cause the fall and rise of many in Israel and to be a sign that will be opposed—and a sword will pierce your own soul—that the thoughts of many hearts may be revealed."

We Christians sometimes live with a fairly deep-seated inferiority complex, if not a spoiled sense of jealousy over the leisurely success we see happening in unbelievers. The psalmist Asaph, for example—boy, you've got to love his inspired honesty—confessed to being pretty bummed out about how his life was stacking up to the ungodly.

On his side of the scorecard: affliction, punishment, not much to show for his daily duties and disciplines. On the *other*: full tables of food, carefree lifestyles, and "an easy time until they die" (Ps. 73:4).

Or at least that's how it seemed in the middle of an average day for Asaph, when work was hard and his shoulders were tired.

But there was one place he could go to get his head screwed back on right, a sacred opportunity he could take to realign and reorient. "When I tried to understand all this," he said, "it seemed hopeless until I entered God's sanctuary. Then I understood" (Ps. 73:16–17).

When quieted in God's presence, he was able to realize afresh that this path which often seems so blind and impassable to our human eyes is not really what it appears. Though the Spirit guides us down trails we may not know or feel confident about, they are passageways he has already blazed through like a warrior, stirring up his "zeal like a soldier," shouting, roaring, ultimately prevailing over all our obstacles and enemies (Isa. 42:13).

So lifting up his downcast eyes from the ground, feeling a heavenly breeze kiss his face, Asaph remembered again that God was leading him to places more filling than any banquet dinner, more fun than any night on the town.

> READ
> PSALM 73:21–28

"As for me, God's presence is my good" (Ps. 73:28), this one who leads me on to glory.

RAIN OR SHINE

We can count on God's loving guidance the rest of our lives— even in times of intense trouble and suffering. PSALM 107 speaks of those who had spent long seasons in the wilderness, nights locked up in prison, endless days of storm at sea. Yet the Spirit "guided them to the harbor they longed for" (v. 30). They weren't left to thrash it out themselves, nor were they doomed to suffer forever. God's hand carried them through.

His guidance even prevails through times of failure. David's expressions captured in Psalm 139 are certainly worshipful enough— "Where can I go to escape Your Spirit? Where can I flee from Your presence" (v. 7). But they seem to be words learned through hard experience, periods when he really *had* wished he could find a place behind God's back, slinking away, hoping the Lord wouldn't notice. Yet *"even there* Your hand will lead me; Your right hand will hold on to me" (v. 10).

We children of God can be totally assured that his Spirit's guidance is there when we need it . . . perhaps even if we don't want it.

READ
EXODUS 15:11–13

ALL THE WAY HOME

Certainly his guidance comes to us most clearly and directly when we're walking faithfully with him through even our most ordinary moments, times when we could easily be tempted to tell the Spirit to take the day off if he wants.

When those prophetic words later used by Christ on the cross become ours each day—"Into Your hand I entrust my spirit" (Ps. 31:5) —that's when we're in the most confident place to discern his leading. When our minds and hearts are routinely accustomed to *thinking* his way, it's no stretch at all to ascertain how to walk his way.

But if this matter of the Spirit's guidance still seems sketchy to you—as if it makes nice sermon material but falls pretty flat between most other hours of operation—receive this as your assignment:

Start asking people who've lived with the Lord for forty, sixty, eighty years if his Spirit has been faithful to guide them through the circuitous journeys of life. See if, as you speak to them, they won't "go around Zion, encircle it; count its towers, note its ramparts; tour its citadels . . . tell a future generation: 'This God, our God forever and ever—He will lead us eternally'" (Ps. 48:12–14).

READ
1 SAMUEL 16:6–13

Indeed, he will.

DIG IN

The life of Simeon isn't given much airtime in the Bible. But the part we do get to see in Luke 2 is a picture of being Spirit led.

"THIS MAN WAS RIGHTEOUS AND DEVOUT . . . AND THE HOLY SPIRIT WAS ON HIM" (v. 25). What is it about being "devout" that makes the Spirit's guidance so much more likely to show up?

....

....

....

....

....

"GUIDED BY THE SPIRIT, HE ENTERED THE TEMPLE COMPLEX" (v. 27). Does the Holy Spirit really take an interest in minor details like this? How involved is he in our little decisions?

....

....

....

....

....

"HIS FATHER AND MOTHER WERE AMAZED AT WHAT WAS BEING SAID ABOUT HIM" (v. 33). Simeon's words came down with weight and gravity. When has that happened to you?

....

....

....

....

....

Experiencing God the Spirit Over and Over Again

1. The Spirit is a gift from the Father.

2. The Spirit exposes and convicts us of sin.

3. The Spirit renews, restores, and refreshes.

4. The Spirit sets us apart for special service.

5. The Spirit indwells those who belong to him.

6. The Spirit gives us guidance and direction.

    When seen through the Spirit's eyes, each day can become an adventure in service and ministry. Every moment is part of a cohesive plan held together by his divine wisdom and lived out through hearts, hands, and feet being trained to react more smoothly each day to his voice. Inside of this is freedom and meaning . . . and the fun of being a Christian.

7. The Spirit empowers and emboldens us.

8. The Spirit gives us insight into God's plans.

9. The Spirit can be grieved and rebelled against.

10. The Spirit instructs us in the will of God.

11. The Spirit moves and repositions his people.

12. The Spirit unites the church in mission.

13. The Spirit fills us with joy and worship.

14. The Spirit endures with us to the end.

Pray About

- Your readiness to respond to the Holy Spirit's direction.
- Your hunger for the Word and its reliable themes of truth.
- Everyday opportunities to practice your faith and trust.

SEVEN
POWERFUL
WORDS

sk pastors and other leaders to tell you what's missing in their churches today—the one or two things they have the hardest time motivating in their members—and they'll probably mention these the most often: *prayer* and *personal evangelism*.

Sure, many other things might be listed there too. *Giving*—although money is sometimes not as hard for us to part with as five minutes of quiet worship in the morning. *Service*—though there's usually somebody who can be guilted into cooking another meal or helping out in the nursery.

But there aren't enough workshops and reminder postcards in the world that can empower us over the long haul to seek God and to share our faith. The only way we'll ever get any better at this—especially the witnessing part—is for us finally to start trusting in the power of the Holy Spirit.

That's because declaring the gospel is not really about techniques or expertise, about formulas and probabilities. It's about loving people enough really to listen to what they're saying and trusting the Spirit enough for us to open up and let him do the talking.

Holy Spirit, where I have failed to share, I take all the blame. But as you speak through me, I will give you all the glory.

I wrote the first narrative, Theophilus, about all that Jesus began to do and teach until the day He was taken up, after *He had given orders through the Holy Spirit to the apostles* whom He had chosen. After He had suffered, He also presented Himself alive to them by many convincing proofs, appearing to them during 40 days and speaking about the kingdom of God.

While He was together with them, He commanded them not to leave Jerusalem, but to wait for the Father's promise. "This," He said, "is what you heard from Me; for John baptized with water, but *you will be baptized with the Holy Spirit not many days from now."*

So when they had come together, they asked Him, "Lord, at this time are You restoring the kingdom to Israel?"

He said to them, "It is not for you to know times or periods that the Father has set by His own authority. But *you will receive power when the Holy Spirit has come upon you,* and you will be My witnesses in Jerusalem, in all Judea and Samaria, and to the ends of the earth."

It's altogether fine and good to seek the Spirit's power in overcoming a sinful habit, in helping to endure a tough loss, or in getting through a particularly draining ordeal. But there is no doubt that when the Scripture talks about our need for receiving the Holy Spirit's might and muscle, his main reason for supplying it is to help us tell others what God has done for us in Christ.

Now our first response to this disclosure, which for some of us may border on utter panic, reveals one of the main reasons the Spirit's power is so essential to our evangelistic efforts. Most of us are aware that when it comes to talking with authority about spiritual matters, our range of knowledge feels far too incomplete. We're a lot more comfortable staying on subjects such as the weather, the

California mud slides, or the good price we got on towels last week at Wal-Mart.

So it's OK to admit it—our human fear is why we need Holy Spirit power!

But even someone as naturally bold and articulate as the apostle Paul sensed deeply his dependence on the Spirit's strength. For him the problem wasn't that he feared being short on things to say but that he might say too much, that he might become so enamored with his own reasoning that he lost all sensitivity to what the Spirit needed done at that moment.

Yes, even those who are spry and scholarly are just as much in need of God's power to witness as the shy and struggling.

> READ
> 1 CORINTHIANS
> 2:1–5

TRUTH ON DEMAND

But no matter which side of that fence you live on, his words are available to us all.

Jesus said, "Whenever they bring you before synagogues and rulers and authorities"—or airplane passengers, a next-door neighbor, or your brother-in-law—"don't worry about how you should defend yourselves or what you should say. For the Holy Spirit will teach you at that very hour what must be said" (LUKE 12:11–12). Even if it doesn't sound particularly profound at the time, it will still be "the Spirit of your Father" speaking through you (MATT. 10:20) directly to a person's need.

That's not to say we can spend all our time analyzing NFL draft choices or reading Internet news blogs and expect just to automatically start sharing coherent, biblical truth whenever the opportunity presents itself. This promise of power is not an excuse to be a spiritual goof-off.

But for those who deliberately stay active in Bible study, keeping close to God in their minds and hearts, intentionally listening for people who are asking serious questions or exposing honest need, the Spirit's words will indeed rise to the surface at just the right time, in just the right way, and with just the right expression. Try it and see.

READ
ACTS 4:23–31

BUILDING ON FAITH

Actually, though, the Spirit has far more than words alone to supply us. His desire is to fuel our *whole lives* until they glow and illuminate with God's life-changing reality.

The Old Testament prophets understood this. Haggai, for example, addressed the bulk of his prophecy to those who had returned to Jerusalem after many generations in exile. Though they had come back with high hopes, nothing was coming easy for them. Most notably, the house of the Lord—Solomon's marvelous temple—still lay in ruins, having been savagely destroyed by the Babylonians years before on a terror trip through Israel's heartland. But there was no money now to build, no time, no energy. It took everything they could muster just to try scratching a living out of deserted, neglected ground.

Haggai, however, had a strong word from God for his countrymen: "My Spirit is present among you; don't be afraid" (2:5).

Trying to resurrect a temple would require more energy and resources than they currently had in reserve. *But that, in fact, was the whole point.* As God supplied, as they eagerly obeyed, "the final glory of this house" would be "greater than the first" (2:9)—"not by strength or by might, but by My Spirit" (ZECH. 4:6). And all the nations on earth would know it.

READ
HAGGAI 2:1–9

Truly we are weak, but he is strong. We should not be sorry for the first or ever doubt the second.

DIG IN

Jesus announced to his disciples in Acts 1 that everything they'd ever need would be theirs through the Holy Spirit.

"HE HAD GIVEN ORDERS THROUGH THE HOLY SPIRIT TO THE APOSTLES" (V. 2). Jesus himself relied on the Spirit to accomplish his work. How do we practice that kind of dependence?

....
....
....
....
....

"YOU WILL BE BAPTIZED WITH THE HOLY SPIRIT NOT MANY DAYS FROM NOW" (V. 5). When the fire fell, everyone knew something special had happened. When do others see that in us?

....
....
....
....
....

"YOU WILL RECEIVE POWER WHEN THE HOLY SPIRIT HAS COME UPON YOU" (V. 8). The Spirit's power is expressly designed for witnessing. How can you begin to appropriate his courage?

....
....
....
....
....

Experiencing God the Spirit
Over and Over Again

1. The Spirit is a gift from the Father.

2. The Spirit exposes and convicts us of sin.

3. The Spirit renews, restores, and refreshes.

4. The Spirit sets us apart for special service.

5. The Spirit indwells those who belong to him.

6. The Spirit gives us guidance and direction.

7. The Spirit empowers and emboldens us.

   Those who try turning the Spirit's blessings inward on themselves find—much to their surprise—that such gorging is like trying to drink from a fire hose. Perhaps the first sign of true spiritual maturity is when we finally understand that his power blesses us best as it passes through us to others, on its mission of bringing honor to him.

8. The Spirit gives us insight into God's plans.

9. The Spirit can be grieved and rebelled against.

10. The Spirit instructs us in the will of God.

11. The Spirit moves and repositions his people.

12. The Spirit unites the church in mission.

13. The Spirit fills us with joy and worship.

14. The Spirit endures with us to the end.

Pray About

- People in your life who you know are in need of Christ.
- The courage to put all your trust in the Spirit's power.
- Wanting God to speak to you more through his Word.

EIGHT

GENTLE WHISPERS

Not too long ago the pastor of our former church made the long drive to Nashville to participate in the baptism of our younger daughter, as well as to preach during the Sunday morning worship service. It had been six or eight months since we'd seen him. We'd talked with him only a few times in between.

But as he began to deliver his message, it was clearly more than just his familiar voice and tone that resonated with my family and me. Our move from the country back into the city had been a good one in many respects, but we had also left much behind—the home where our kids had spent the bulk of their growing-up years—all their elaborate childhood adventures in the nearby hayfields and pastures, pretending to be subsisting on nothing but honeysuckles and berries, combing the surrounding acres for water and shelter.

Oh, and the quiet. My, how we miss the quiet.

Yet the words of his sermon that day, as well as each hymn selection and Scripture verse, spoke of new beginnings, of God's plan that survives through it all.

There's no way he could've known all we needed to hear that day. But the Spirit did. And our friend had been listening.

Spirit of God, make our hearts open enough to hear what you have to say. And never hold back from saying what we need to hear.

Among the mature we do speak a wisdom, but not a wisdom of this age, or of the rulers of this age, who are coming to nothing. On the contrary, *we speak God's hidden wisdom in a mystery*, which God predestined before the ages for our glory. None of the rulers of this age knew it, for if they had known it, they would not have crucified the Lord of glory. But as it is written, "What no eye has seen and no ear has heard, and what has never come into a man's heart, is what God has prepared for those who love Him."

Now God has revealed them to us by the Spirit, for *the Spirit searches everything, even the deep things of God*. For who among men knows the concerns of a man except the spirit of the man that is in him? In the same way, no one knows the concerns of God except the Spirit of God. Now we have not received the spirit of the world, but the Spirit who is from God, *in order to know what has been freely given to us by God*. We also speak these things, not in words taught by human wisdom, but in those taught by the Spirit, explaining spiritual things to spiritual people.

It's good that we don't know everything. Yes, we've seen the emaciated faces and bloated bellies of poverty on relief-fund infomercials. We've seen the earth-moving devastation of overseas tsunamis and Gulf Coast hurricanes. We've seen a young mother collapse against a column on her front porch, her child thought to be abducted by a drifting psychopath, her life unraveling at the hands of the unthinkable.

We've seen these things in isolation, usually from a distance, through the lens of the morning news, all the while maintaining the stomach to lift a cereal spoon to our mouths.

But if we could somehow feel all the accumulated grief, pain, and panic felt by millions in our world this very minute, our hearts couldn't bear the weight. Our head would swim, our breathing would stop, we'd likely explode.

Neither could we deal with knowing all the answers to all our questions. In fact, our brains can hardly process the information we already have as it is! Besides, if we feel the need to protect our children from various bits of knowledge that we don't consider them yet ready for, what makes us think that we—mere children ourselves—could handle everything there is to know?

And so God wisely, lovingly, parentally shields us from those things that would overload us, choosing instead to reveal everything we *need* to know one piece at a time . . . through the unfolding presence of his Holy Spirit.

> READ
> PSALM 119:130–132

ALL EARS

So rather than bewailing God's silence, accusing him of holding out on us, we should instead celebrate his protective provision, while seeking at the same time to cultivate minds and hearts that are hungry to hear his thoughts. For he *does* yearn to tell us more, to have our full attention long enough to speak in whole paragraphs and complete sentences.

As Paul said in some of the verses later on in 1 Corinthians 2, it is within our grace-given ability as spiritually transformed people to "evaluate everything" (v. 15), to walk with Holy Spirit discernment into any situation, our hearts carefully attuned to see much more than meets the eye.

Why don't we, then? It's because we insist on keeping enough of our "natural man" around to entertain us on days when God's not floating our boat. Therefore, we lose the capacity to distinguish truth from "foolishness" (v. 14). Flesh and blood simply cannot locate the frequency the Spirit uses to transmit his truth into our lives.

So we miss his signal. We keep things on the surface. We settle for small talk. And when we do, we resign ourselves to living in spiritual crisis, conflicted, wanting to know more yet not really willing to listen.

But "if our hearts do not condemn [us]"—if we are letting him grow the disciplined fruits of purity and simplicity in our lives— "we have confidence before God, and can receive whatever we ask of Him . . . from the Spirit He has given us" (1 JOHN 3:21–22, 24).

READ
EPHESIANS 3:16–19

GOOD LISTENERS

That's not to say that this ever gets totally easy. But it does get easier "for those whose *senses have been trained* to distinguish between good and evil" (HEB. 5:14)—between natural and spiritual, between the readily obvious and the extraordinarily eternal.

It gets easier for those who become one with the Word, who regularly listen for the Spirit to point out a passage here, to highlight a phrase there, to enliven a certain section as they read or study or hear it proclaimed.

It gets easier for those who become people of ongoing prayer, who pray when the car is warming up, when the potatoes are baking, when they're dusting the furniture or cutting the grass.

It gets easier for those who ask the Lord to help them read the news with spiritual glasses, to listen for spiritual clues in casual conversation, to spend time with people who are practicing the Spirit's presence even late in the afternoon on Fridays.

The only thing that never gets any easier is trying to pull this off part-time, trying to *act* spiritual when called upon but not *being* spiritual when the curtain's down. The Spirit has some mighty things to say when we're ready to listen.

READ
ACTS 20:22–24

DIG IN

Some people mistake Paul's boldness as arrogance. But in 1 Corinthians 2, you see where all his confidence lay.

"WE SPEAK GOD'S HIDDEN WISDOM IN A MYSTERY" (V. 7). It shouldn't surprise us that our perspectives don't make sense to everybody. What is our motive for wanting them to?

....

....

....

....

....

"THE SPIRIT SEARCHES EVERYTHING, EVEN THE DEEP THINGS OF GOD" (V. 10). Think on that phrase: "the deep things of God." How bad do you really want to plunge in for that?

....

....

....

....

....

"IN ORDER TO KNOW WHAT HAS BEEN FREELY GIVEN TO US BY GOD" (V. 12). Yes, we can begin to understand these things already. What can we do to understand them even better?

....

....

....

....

....

Experiencing God the Spirit Over and Over Again

1. The Spirit is a gift from the Father.

2. The Spirit exposes and convicts us of sin.

3. The Spirit renews, restores, and refreshes.

4. The Spirit sets us apart for special service.

5. The Spirit indwells those who belong to him.

6. The Spirit gives us guidance and direction.

7. The Spirit empowers and emboldens us.

8. The Spirit gives us insight into God's plans.
   He knows the plans he has for you—"plans for [your] welfare, not for disaster, to give you a future and a hope." Therefore, the Spirit asks you to "call to Me and come and pray to Me, and I will listen to you. You will seek Me and find Me when you search for Me with all your heart" (Jer. 29:11–13), when you listen with a spirit that's willing to obey what you hear.

9. The Spirit can be grieved and rebelled against.

10. The Spirit instructs us in the will of God.

11. The Spirit moves and repositions his people.

12. The Spirit unites the church in mission.

13. The Spirit fills us with joy and worship.

14. The Spirit endures with us to the end.

Pray About

- Your attitude toward the seeming, sometime silence of God.
- Your willingness to seek him—to really and truly seek him.
- What you would likely do with the Spirit's information.

NINE

OUCH,
THAT HURTS

Most students of Scripture are well familiar with the troubles the Israelites had in trying to keep one foot planted faithfully in front of the other. There was the golden calf incident, for example. Complaining about the water. Complaining about the manna. Complaining about not having a king like everybody else.

You know the stories.

In keeping with the natural fallout from such forgetfulness, of course, they met with a lot of consequences over the years. Diseases. Delays. Defeats and derisions. The hard discipline of God. And though it was every bit warranted, the hardships they endured weren't easy for the Lord to watch. In fact, in one of the Bible's most tender passages, Isaiah wrote that "in all their suffering, He suffered" (ISA. 63:9).

When they hurt, he hurt. When they grieved, he grieved.

This tips us off early on to an interesting aspect of God's character. He is not some distant deity, unfazed by what happens between the tree lines of our lives. He can hurt. He can feel. He can be wounded, mistreated, and heartsick.

We've seen it in the Father. We certainly saw it in the Son. We still see it in the Spirit.

Holy Spirit, it helps me to know that you can hurt. May this knowledge help me keep from hurting you myself.

A man named Ananias, with Sapphira his wife, sold a piece of property. However, he kept back part of the proceeds with his wife's knowledge, and brought a portion of it and laid it at the apostles' feet.

Then Peter said, "Ananias, *why has Satan filled your heart to lie to the Holy Spirit* and keep back part of the proceeds from the field? Wasn't it yours while you possessed it? And after it was sold, wasn't it at your disposal? Why is it that you planned this thing in your heart? *You have not lied to men but to God!*" When he heard these words, Ananias dropped dead, and a great fear came on all who heard. The young men got up, wrapped his body, carried him out, and buried him.

There was an interval of about three hours; then his wife came in, not knowing what had happened. "Tell me," Peter asked her, "did you sell the field for this price?"

"Yes," she said, "for that price."

Then Peter said to her, "*Why did you agree to test the Spirit of the Lord?* Look! The feet of those who have buried your husband are at the door, and they will carry you out!"

I've been trying really hard not to write these studies in your typical three-point sermon outline. But maybe the best way to tackle this particular topic is to go back to the old standby, breaking down a few of the specific ways we fall guilty in the "grieving" area.

The first and most obvious way is through *failing to maintain a pure lifestyle.*

Certainly, purity involves a lot more than sexual cleanness, but the Bible does include it so often in its lists of egregious sins that it's worth warning one another about. I mean, who knew the Bible could be so far ahead of its time, touching on a subject that's as modern-day as Saturday night television and halftime at the Super Bowl?

"For this is God's will, your sanctification: that you abstain from sexual immorality.... The person who rejects this does not reject man, but God, who also gives you His Holy Spirit" (1 THESS. 4:3, 8).

To sin is to "reject" his authority in our lives, to treat him like an intruding imposter, to elevate our own idols into positions of prominence, strong-arming the Spirit like revolutionaries executing an overthrow.

And it hurts him. Not in a sulking way. Not in a see-if-I-care kind of snippiness. Not in a way that makes him feel the need to defend his Word, but rather forcing him to assume the undesirable role of "avenger" (1 THESS. 4:6), seeking to correct the short circuits in our character before we go beyond merely hurting ourselves and start taking other people with us.

> READ
> COLOSSIANS 3:5—7

FAMILY FEUDS

Speaking of which, another way we offend the Holy Spirit is by *treating one another badly.*

The context of Paul's familiar statement in Ephesians 4:30 — "Don't grieve God's Holy Spirit, who sealed you for the day of redemption"—includes a bam-bam combination of direct assaults against "bitterness, anger and wrath, insult and slander" (v. 31).

In other words, let your sin leak out onto other people enough, and you'll have more than your own mess to clean up. Like most moms or dads would say, you can do whatever you want to *them*, but don't go picking on their kids. If you've ever tried getting too close to a mockingbird's nest, you find out real quick that the egg protector never takes both eyes off home base.

And so it is with the Holy Spirit, who broods over his people with a parent's brand of protection. He knows that battles across bloodlines do nothing but damage and divide, hammering pockmarks into the unity and mission of the church. When we war with each other, we set ourselves in contention against the Spirit of God,

READ
COLOSSIANS 3:8–10
who will not allow such discord to continue untreated.

THE BIG HEAD

And finally, point number three (if you're still keeping score at home): we insult the Holy Spirit when we use *him to prop up our own pride.*

The most vivid example of this is the story of Simon the sorcerer, found in ACTS 8, a guy who liked to be called "the Great Power of God" (v. 10). But even a grand showman can sometimes have the guts to know when he's licked—like when Philip blew into town at the Spirit's direction, sending demons shrieking off in search of shelter, even returning the paralyzed to their upright positions.

A little later, when Peter and John arrived, Simon "offered them money, saying, 'Give me this power too, so that anyone I lay hands on may receive the Holy Spirit'" (vv. 18–19).

But the Spirit is not for profit. Or for reputation. Or for playing to the crowd. That's why every time a singer loves his key change more than his message, every time a minister starts living for compliments and recognition, every time a writer thinks his clever words exempt him from cultivating Christian character, the Spirit is wounded, insulted, maligned, taken advantage of.

Yet this one whose heart can break at our misbehavior is also the one who can put us back together. For he is willing to suffer but not to leave us forsaken. In order that we grieve him less, he gives us his healing.

READ
HEBREWS 10:26–39

54

DIG IN

We all know the story of Ananias and Sapphira from Acts 5. But we may not know what they're most guilty of.

"WHY HAS SATAN FILLED YOUR HEART TO LIE TO THE HOLY SPIRIT . . .?" (v. 3). Notice who's involved here. We know how Satan feels about untruth. Why is it so biting to the Holy Spirit?

....
....
....
....
....

"YOU HAVE NOT LIED TO MEN BUT TO GOD" (v. 4). What veils this truth from our eyes? What would help us live with a more ongoing awareness of how near and present the Spirit is?

....
....
....
....
....

"WHY DID YOU AGREE TO TEST THE SPIRIT OF THE LORD?" (v. 9). Think about the danger and audacity in what she's being accused of here. In what ways can we be just as daring?

....
....
....
....
....

Experiencing God the Spirit Over and Over Again

1. The Spirit is a gift from the Father.
2. The Spirit exposes and convicts us of sin.
3. The Spirit renews, restores, and refreshes.
4. The Spirit sets us apart for special service.
5. The Spirit indwells those who belong to him.
6. The Spirit gives us guidance and direction.
7. The Spirit empowers and emboldens us.
8. The Spirit gives us insight into God's plans.
9. The Spirit can be grieved and rebelled against.

   A God who could not be disobeyed would be more tyrant than shepherd. And a God who didn't hurt when we sinned would be more slaveholder than Father. His Spirit lives too close not to feel it when we ignore him or rebel against him. But he also lives too close to overlook it, to turn the other way, to be content until he's shown us what sin can do and how to stop it.

10. The Spirit instructs us in the will of God.
11. The Spirit moves and repositions his people.
12. The Spirit unites the church in mission.
13. The Spirit fills us with joy and worship.
14. The Spirit endures with us to the end.

Pray About

- Things you're doing right now to wound the Holy Spirit.
- A regular awareness of the Spirit's nearness and love.
- Joining with others to cut down on dead behavior.

TEN
BACK TO THE
BLACKBOARD

When we count on the Holy Spirit to instruct us in his will, we're usually talking about his will *for us*—our work, our family, our church, our own stuff. And that's perfectly all right because every child of God needs to know his will for these things.

Yes, he *does* have a plan for our job and vocation. He *does* have a plan for our marriage, our children. He *does* have a plan for our church and its ministries.

And we do well to find out what that is and to walk in it.

But as Henry Blackaby, author of *Experiencing God*, has helped millions of us see over the years, the best question to ask of the Holy Spirit is not, "What is your will for me?" but simply, "What is your will?" That's because inside this enormous question—and inside its even more panoramic answer—lies the eternal mission of God that frames our workaday worlds in ultimate meaning and purpose.

A lot more is taking place in our lives than just what gets logged on the calendar or posted on the refrigerator. The Spirit wants to show us what that is. And class starts up again in the morning.

Holy Spirit, help me want to do your will as much as I want to know your will. Make me, I pray, a better student.

You did not abandon them in the wilderness because of Your great compassion. During the day the pillar of cloud never turned away from them, guiding them on their journey. And during the night the pillar of fire illuminated the way they should go. *You sent your good Spirit to instruct them.* You did not withhold Your manna from their mouths, and You gave them water for their thirst. You provided for them in the wilderness 40 years and they lacked nothing. . . .

But they were disobedient and rebelled against You. They flung Your law behind their backs and killed Your prophets who warned them to turn back to You. . . . You warned them to turn back to Your law, but they acted arrogantly and would not obey Your commandments. They sinned against Y*our ordinances,* by which *a person will live if he does them.* They stubbornly resisted, stiffened their necks, and would not obey.

You were patient with them for many years, and *Your Spirit warned them through Your prophets,* but they would not listen. Therefore, You handed them over to the surrounding peoples. However, in Your abundant compassion, You did not destroy them or abandon them, for You are a gracious and compassionate God.

The reconstituted nation of Israel was just getting back on its feet after many years lost to captivity, and its leaders were feeling the need to take the people back to square one. Reminds me of the old Vince Lombardi quote, when he decided his Green Bay Packers needed retooling after an especially sloppy loss. Assuming his central spot in the locker room, hoisting a pigskin into the air, the legendary coach began his refresher course by announcing to his troops, "Gentlemen, this is a football."

Back to basics. That's why Nehemiah 9 is pure highlight material, like a war documentary on The History Channel. It's a look back at centuries of Israelite lore that had likely been lost on many of the listeners in attendance. Although it reads with almost shopworn familiarity as *we* skim through it, much of it was probably headline news to those who heard it shouted that day from the speaker's stand.

Among its more important aspects was how it described the will of God—a plan conceived in his heart from the time he "created the heavens" (v. 6), a plan for his people that included an everlasting covenant and a promised land.

Along the way this plan required a lot of direction on God's end as it played itself out in their lives, an equal-parts mixture of coaching and rescue, of both warnings and encouragement. It meant giving them pointers ahead of time, as well as midstream corrections where deemed necessary.

Yet even when they ignored his instruction, the Spirit continued to teach, showing them how to recover, repent, and find restoration to remain in his will.

They didn't follow him perfectly. None of us do. Yet the Spirit kept reenrolling them. And his plan stayed the same. His plan stayed big—even bigger than their disobedience.

> READ
> PSALM 143:7–10

BACK TO SCHOOL

God's people continued to need his teaching as time roared into the New Testament. Imagine the juggling act, for example, required of the early church leaders, dealing with all the dynamics that swirled around their new world order.

Jews who still wanted God without too much Jesus on the side. Gentiles who showed up without baggage but also without a lot of spiritual sense. Old-timers who felt entitled. Newcomers who felt enlightened.

Anyone seen the Tylenol?

But when push came to shove—and nearly to blows—over the circumcision issue (whether or not Gentile converts should be required to submit to this Jewish rite of fellowship), the apostles and elders called time-out and convened in Jerusalem.

They prayed. They heard reports from the field. They read from the ancient Scriptures. And when it all settled out, "it was the Holy Spirit's decision—and ours" (ACTS 15:28) to nix circumcision as the cost of admission. The Spirit made clear what he wanted done, and his people made sure they stayed in step with his wishes.

READ
ISAIAH 48:16−18

EAGER TO LEARN

Today *we're* the students in the Spirit's classroom. But our lives are awfully busy. Our options are more numerous than any generation before us. We sometimes squirm in our seats and find ourselves staring out the window.

But deep down we really do want our lives to mesh with the plans he set in motion before the beginning of time. We want to believe that there's nothing truly routine in a believer's day, that there's more involved in our decision to accept a new responsibility or contribute money to a new missionary—or even check out a new book from the library—than the surface issues that go along with it.

We need to know that "the Spirit of truth" will show us his will if we ask him. We need to know that he's been sent to us by the Father to "guide [us] into all the truth." We need to know that he doesn't "speak on His own" but tells us only what he hears from the heart of God himself. And we need to know that his purpose is to "glorify" Christ, just as we want our purpose to be (JOHN 16:13−14).

So teach us, Holy Spirit. Give us ears to hear and minds to understand. And legs and feet to live it out, to walk in the direction of your perfect will.

READ
JOHN 15:26−27

DIG IN

Israel's national confession of sin, recorded in Nehemiah 9, was also a reminder of how the Spirit's teaching works.

"YOU SENT YOUR GOOD SPIRIT TO INSTRUCT THEM" (V. 20). We often put "good" and "instruction" in opposite categories. But what makes the Spirit's teaching really good?

....

....

....

....

....

"YOUR ORDINANCES . . . A PERSON WILL LIVE IF HE DOES THEM" (V. 29). Certainly we're no longer under the law's demands. But what can we still learn from its instructions?

....

....

....

....

....

"YOUR SPIRIT WARNED THEM THROUGH YOUR PROPHETS" (V. 30). Warning is in many ways an expression of love. How have his red flags been kind and helpful to you in the past?

....

....

....

....

....

Experiencing God the Spirit Over and Over Again

1. The Spirit is a gift from the Father.

2. The Spirit exposes and convicts us of sin.

3. The Spirit renews, restores, and refreshes.

4. The Spirit sets us apart for special service.

5. The Spirit indwells those who belong to him.

6. The Spirit gives us guidance and direction.

7. The Spirit empowers and emboldens us.

8. The Spirit gives us insight into God's plans.

9. The Spirit can be grieved and rebelled against.

10. The Spirit instructs us in the will of God.

    I'd say most of us live unsure about what the particulars of God's will are. But we really need to trust both him and his Word enough to believe that by letting him speak and by listening in prayer, we can walk confidently into the unknowns and be assured of his direction. This is not just me trying to sound spiritual. This is God's promise. And we can count on him.

11. The Spirit moves and repositions his people.

12. The Spirit unites the church in mission.

13. The Spirit fills us with joy and worship.

14. The Spirit endures with us to the end.

Pray About

- Specific areas where you need to know his will and plan.
- A wider-open mind that seeks his kingdom over yours.
- People you need to be regularly praying for and with.

ELEVEN
MOVE 'EM OUT

Stephanie had just put the phone down. Whether she actually got it hung up or not, she wasn't sure. Actually, she wasn't sure of *anything* at the moment. The call had come from her seventy-six-year-old mom, five hundred miles away, where her dad had just gotten the results of his latest medical test. Cancer. Everywhere.

Janeen had gotten through at the dentist earlier than she expected but not early enough to go all the way home before picking up her kids at school. She wasn't often in that part of town at this time of day. In fact, she'd been forced to reschedule her appointment from two weeks ago, and this had been the first opening she could take. But since she had a few extra minutes, she thought she might swing by and see her friend Stephanie and find out how her dad's doing.

Stephanie really needed Janeen that day. At exactly 2:18 in the afternoon. Needed a friend who could hug her close, cry with her, and start praying that God would do something about this.

The Holy Spirit knew it too. That's why Janeen was there. In Stephanie's neighborhood. Killing time. And believe it or not, following orders.

Holy Spirit, I give you full authority to move me anywhere you need me to go, anytime you can use me there.

ACTS 8:26–31, 35–36, 39

An angel of the Lord spoke to Philip: *"Get up and go south to the road that goes down from Jerusalem to desert Gaza."* So he got up and went. There was an Ethiopian man, a eunuch and high official of Candace, queen of the Ethiopians, who was in charge of her whole treasury. He had come to worship in Jerusalem and was sitting in his chariot on his way home, reading the prophet Isaiah aloud.

The Spirit told Philip, "Go and join that chariot."

When Philip ran up to it, he heard him reading the prophet Isaiah, and said, "Do you understand what you're reading?"

"How can I," he said, "unless someone guides me?" So he invited Philip to come up and sit with him. . . .

Philip proceeded to tell him the good news about Jesus, beginning from that Scripture.

As they were traveling down the road, they came to some water. The eunuch said, "Look, there's water! What would keep me from being baptized?". . . When they came up out of the water, *the Spirit of the Lord carried Philip away,* and the eunuch did not see him any longer. But he went on his way rejoicing.

I absolutely love the way my friend Ken Hemphill interprets Exodus 19:5, a verse that listens in as God says to Israel, "You will be My own possession out of all the peoples." In his book *EKG: The Heartbeat of God*, he notes that the Hebrew word translated "possession" refers to property that could be relocated—like money or jewelry—as opposed to real estate or something.

This made Israel (to use Ken's term) a "movable possession"— an asset that God could reposition on his own terms in order to meet his desired purpose.

So pick your person in the Bible, and see if you don't see this happening with historic regularity. Joseph, sold by his belligerent brothers into slavery in Egypt (GEN. 37:28). Ezekiel, time after time, "lifted . . . up" and "brought" by the Spirit to a new place of revelation (EZEK. 43:5). Peter, sent "with no doubts at all" to the house of Cornelius, the Gentile (ACTS 10:20).

Abraham. Jacob. Moses. Joshua. Ruth. Nehemiah. Esther. This is the pattern established by the Spirit throughout the Scripture—taking his people from one place to another, transporting all the investment he had made in them up to that point and planting it in new ground where its fruit was needed the most.

READ
ESTHER 4:13–14

TRAVEL GUIDE

We continue to see this happening in our lives today.

A man is offered a job two states away. He prays and prays about what to do, weighing all the obvious elements of salary expectations and professional opportunities. Yet at the same time, he's reminded by the Spirit to be consciously aware that the Lord may have much more involved in this move than the things that show up on a pro-and-con list.

A family begins badly outgrowing the two-bedroom, one-bath house they bought long before they discovered that child number three (on the way) will actually be numbers three and four. But whether they realize it or not, the best house for them won't merely be the one with the right square-footage and the place for a tire swing but the one that situates them next door to a couple who's *also* expecting twins . . . and in need of a Savior.

We could never figure this stuff out on our own. But that's what makes our walk with Christ so perfectly freeing—if we'll let it be—because his Spirit has already figured all this out for us. Our job is just to scoot over, let him drive, and enjoy the scenery.

Interestingly, in fact, the Spirit can even do this in reverse. In one particular travelogue portion from the book of Acts, Paul and Timothy were going ahead with every intention of working their way one by one through the various provinces of Asia. "When they came to Mysia," however, "they tried to go into Bithynia, but the Spirit of Jesus did not allow them" (16:7). The guiding hand of the Spirit that was moving them throughout the region was also *preventing* them from going to places where he didn't want them to go.

That's the kind of travel agent we need—one who not only knows the best way to move us from one place to the next but also

READ
ACTS 16:8–10

knows which places would take us out of his will and, therefore, cause us nothing but trouble.

HEAR ANYTHING?

Some people who testify that the Spirit told them to go here or go there were more likely just a little too pumped up on caffeine. We know that happens. We do need to be careful before throwing the weight of God behind our own hunches.

But having said that, the Bible is clear that our relationship with the Spirit is one that invites his supervision.

In practice, I don't think it's as much about having a thought bubble appear over our heads as it is adopting a conscious, ongoing awareness of our own availability to him. It means staying in constant contact, regularly reminding ourselves to be listening for his sense of direction, remembering from the outset who's really in charge of this day. Those are the kinds of practices that make us able to hear him. Fasting. Praying. Occasionally choosing quiet conversation over another Blockbuster night.

And then when he speaks, we move it.

READ
ACTS 21:3–14

DIG IN

Philip's experience in Acts 8 is more than just a historical vignette but a testimony to what we can continue to expect.

"GET UP AND GO SOUTH TO THE ROAD THAT GOES DOWN FROM JERUSALEM" (V. 26). Has the Spirit ever been that specific with you? Would you agree or disagree with whether he does that?

....
....
....
....
....

"THE SPIRIT TOLD PHILIP, 'GO AND JOIN THAT CHARIOT'" (V. 29). Philip was obviously aware of his surroundings. What kinds of things do we miss by not being spiritually observant?

....
....
....
....
....

"THE SPIRIT OF THE LORD CARRIED PHILIP AWAY" (V. 39). God seems to have seasons for his people. What are the implications of this? How does this change our life expectations?

....
....
....
....
....

Experiencing God the Spirit Over and Over Again

1. The Spirit is a gift from the Father.
2. The Spirit exposes and convicts us of sin.
3. The Spirit renews, restores, and refreshes.
4. The Spirit sets us apart for special service.
5. The Spirit indwells those who belong to him.
6. The Spirit gives us guidance and direction.
7. The Spirit empowers and emboldens us.
8. The Spirit gives us insight into God's plans.
9. The Spirit can be grieved and rebelled against.
10. The Spirit instructs us in the will of God.
11. The Spirit moves and repositions his people.

    "Movable possessions." That's what we are in the hand of God. Don't think of it in terms of a chessboard. That's too dungeons-and-dragons feeling. Too militaristic. Besides, this isn't a *game* God's playing with us. This is his love for people, placing us in situations where we can both encourage and *be* encouraged, comfort and be comforted, share and be shared with.

12. The Spirit unites the church in mission.
13. The Spirit fills us with joy and worship.
14. The Spirit endures with us to the end.

Pray About

- Developing the eyes to see where the Spirit is leading you.
- Discerning what he has in mind for you here, in this place.
- How entrenched you may be, unwilling to budge easily.

TWELVE

SAME, ONLY DIFFERENT

It doesn't require a whole lot of dyslexia to misread the word *united* as *untied*. But no matter how small a mix-up it takes to reverse those two little up-and-down letters, the change in meaning is extreme—from "pulled together" to "pulled apart."

The church is the same way. One little statement said out of place or interpreted the wrong way can cause a major disturbance. One little budget cut or salary increase. One little decision that leads to another, and another, until the only good decision left is a painful corrective that's sure to offend somebody, maybe everybody.

Granted, every church has its share of people who haven't sought the Spirit's leadership in their lives since the Carter administration. As a result, there's only so much unity you can expect when some are into this thing with a passion and others just for the pancake breakfasts.

But truly the only thing that has the power to oil the differences between you, me, and all the other square pegs that make up God's church is the ministry of the Holy Spirit. So if we can't get along about something, one of us (at least) has quit wanting his way.

Spirit of Christ, I pray for my church today, asking that you'd give us the grace to realize that it's your church, not ours.

Now there are different gifts, but the same Spirit. There are different ministries, but the same Lord. And there are different activities, but the same God is active in everyone and everything. *A manifestation of the Spirit is given to each person* to produce what is beneficial: to one is given a message of wisdom through the Spirit, to another, a message of knowledge by the same Spirit, to another, faith by the same Spirit, to another, gifts of healing by the one Spirit, to another, the performing of miracles, to another, prophecy, to another, distinguishing between spirits, to another, different kinds of languages, to another, interpretation of languages. But *one and the same Spirit is active in all these,* distributing to each one as He wills. For as the body is one and has many parts, and all the parts of that body, though many, are one body—so also is Christ. For *we were all baptized by one Spirit into one body*—whether Jews or Greeks, whether slaves or free—and we were all made to drink of one Spirit. So the body is not one part but many.

Some people are really good at making small talk with total strangers. (Some, actually, are a little too good. A guy I once sat next to on a flight from Baltimore comes to mind.) But most of us do much better in conversation when we have some kind of reason for connecting, a shared piece of common ground we can both step out on at the same time, like:

"Has your son decided about college yet?"

"Sure been too wet to do much golfing lately."

"I ran into someone the other day who knows you."

But for those of us who've been received into the body of Christ, our primary point of contact with one another no longer needs to be whether we run at the same track, get our firewood from the same guy, or enjoy the same kind of reading. ("Even the *pagans* do that," you can almost hear Jesus saying.)

That's because we now have the "fellowship of the Holy Spirit" to unite us as believers (2 COR. 13:13). And that ought to be our main reason for getting together.

READ
EPHESIANS 4:1–4

SIGNS OF THE SPIRIT

According to Paul's teaching, this "fellowship with the Spirit" should show itself in several different ways inside our church relationships (PHIL. 2:1–2).

"By thinking the same way." This doesn't mean we have to agree totally on every little incidental. But when we're actively seeking the Spirit's leadership, we can learn to let a lot of things go. We can remove the "my way" mentality from our menu and not let our personal tastes poison the experience for everybody.

"Having the same love." Maybe this one is the most convicting because it means asking ourselves what our real love is. Is it work? Is it weekends? Is it turkey hunting? Is it our own down time? The "love" Paul was talking about, of course, was our "first love" of relationship with Jesus (REV. 2:4 KJV)—our love for spiritual things, our love for doing the will of God, our love for encouraging one another by talking about what he's doing in our lives. Until that love is truly our real love, we can't all share the "same love" together.

"Sharing the same feelings." As hard as it is for some of us to believe—and as hard as it can be for any of us to put into practice—the Holy Spirit promises that we can indeed enjoy an attitude and atmosphere of like-mindedness in our church. We can submit to him something as nearly uncontrollable as our own feelings and emotions, and experience his power working through us. That's what the Bible says.

"Focusing on one goal." Imagine what could be immediately demoted from irritant status in our hearts if our only desires were

to worship, serve, and honor Christ. Through the Holy Spirit this miracle really can occur at your church's street address, as well as

READ
EPHESIANS 2:21–22 throughout the town or city where your members live, work, and pitch in together. One goal: the glory of God.

UNITY EATERS

But certainly there are threats to this Holy Spirit harmony: those who refuse to submit to the Spirit's leadership, who don't make him or his will too big a part of their day.

Now most of those who keep the cart upset aren't acting from motives that are deliberately destructive. They feel strongly about their positions and, in their own way, are probably doing what they think is best. But the Bible says that those who "create divisions" are operating out of hearts that are "merely natural, not having the Spirit" (JUDE 19).

This doesn't necessarily mean they're not Christians. Any one of us is more than capable of letting our "natural" man plop itself square in the driver's seat. And every time we do, we assure ourselves an automatic detour from everything the Lord desires to accomplish through us.

But we can pray and seek the Spirit afresh. We can believe the Scriptures when they say that unity is well within his power, even in the most dastardly of congregations. And though it may not happen overnight, we can start seeing some walls come down, and hard feelings being softened, and God returning to his rightful place . . . right in the center of everything.

READ
1 THESSALONIANS 5:23–24

DIG IN

The church is indeed a big tent, as you can see in 1 Corinthians 12, but there's no doubt who's here to run the show.

"A MANIFESTATION OF THE SPIRIT IS GIVEN TO EACH PERSON" (V. 7). No two Christians are alike, but no *one* Christian is without a spiritual gift. Why is this so important?

....
....
....
....
....

"ONE AND THE SAME SPIRIT IS ACTIVE IN ALL THESE" (V. 11). What are some of the most important results and benefits of having an "active" Holy Spirit at work in us?

....
....
....
....
....

"WE WERE ALL BAPTIZED BY ONE SPIRIT INTO ONE BODY" (V. 13). "One" is a crucial number in the church. How does this apply when people have legitimate doctrinal differences?

....
....
....
....
....

Experiencing God the Spirit
Over and Over Again

1. THE SPIRIT IS A GIFT FROM THE FATHER.
2. THE SPIRIT EXPOSES AND CONVICTS US OF SIN.
3. THE SPIRIT RENEWS, RESTORES, AND REFRESHES.
4. THE SPIRIT SETS US APART FOR SPECIAL SERVICE.
5. THE SPIRIT INDWELLS THOSE WHO BELONG TO HIM.
6. THE SPIRIT GIVES US GUIDANCE AND DIRECTION.
7. THE SPIRIT EMPOWERS AND EMBOLDENS US.
8. THE SPIRIT GIVES US INSIGHT INTO GOD'S PLANS.
9. THE SPIRIT CAN BE GRIEVED AND REBELLED AGAINST.
10. THE SPIRIT INSTRUCTS US IN THE WILL OF GOD.
11. THE SPIRIT MOVES AND REPOSITIONS HIS PEOPLE.
12. THE SPIRIT UNITES THE CHURCH IN MISSION.
    Even blood relations—which (depending on our age) only go
    back thirty, fifty, seventy some-odd years—can never create
    the connectedness that occurs when the Holy Spirit draws
    us together in eternal fellowship with Christ. And the bond
    between us only gets tighter as we learn to love him more. He is
    indeed the glue that holds the church together.
13. THE SPIRIT FILLS US WITH JOY AND WORSHIP.
14. THE SPIRIT ENDURES WITH US TO THE END.

PRAY ABOUT

- How your church is doing in the spiritual unity department.
- What you can do to foster a deeper spirit of fellowship.
- A greater love and unity among all believers in Christ.

THIRTEEN

JOY GIVER

I f you've been unable to hold back a smile when reacting to the truth of a Scripture verse, you've got the Holy Spirit to thank for that experience.

Every time the words and music of a favorite hymn, chorus, or choir number has made you want to stand to your feet and lift your hands in worship, you've been brought there—out of yourself and into God's presence—on the powerful wings of the Spirit.

Whenever you've been together in prayer with a handful of friends and closed out the night by sharing coffee and conversation around the kitchen table, you've enjoyed a sense of community created just for you by the Holy Spirit.

Even in times when life wasn't cooperating—but you finally broke through to a place where you could breathe again—the hands that held you and led you out of the darkness came from the firm, eternal grip of God's Spirit. He knows full well how to wrest joy from the tight fist of hardship.

There are many wholesale suppliers of spiritual ice cream and candy, of feel-good moments and flighty infatuations. But true joy is only made by one manufacturer who still delivers right to your door.

Holy Spirit, I could use a little of that today. Help me not to waste my time looking for it anywhere else.

The Seventy returned with joy, saying, "Lord, even the demons submit to us in Your name."

He said to them, "I watched Satan fall from heaven like a lightning flash. Look, I have given you authority to trample on snakes and scorpions and over all the power of the enemy; nothing will ever harm you. However, don't rejoice that the spirits submit to you, but rejoice that your names are written in heaven."

In that same hour He rejoiced in the Holy Spirit and said, "I praise You, Father, Lord of heaven and earth, because You have hidden these things from the wise and the learned and have revealed them to infants. Yes, Father, because this was Your good pleasure. All things have been entrusted to Me by My Father. No one knows who the Son is except the Father, and who the Father is except the Son, and anyone to whom the Son desires to reveal Him."

Then turning to His disciples He said privately, *"The eyes that see the things you see are blessed!* For I tell you that many prophets and kings wanted to see the things you see yet didn't see them; to hear the things you hear yet didn't hear them."

I know it's not the way our minds customarily think, not in today's highly competitive, advertising-based culture. We like to push the benefits of our product, then wait for later (after someone's already bought in and can't bring it back) before they discover that there's some work involved in getting the results they were promised.

Yes, the bleach spray *will* whiten the grout and tile in your bathroom shower but not without some toothbrush scrubbing. The fancy new rug shampoo *will* get the pet stains out of your carpet, but you'll have to get down on your knees to do it.

And so I've deliberately left off this upbeat attribute of the Spirit till near the end of the book because to do otherwise wouldn't be entirely honest or give the whole picture.

People wouldn't understand that his is a *deeper* joy than they're thinking of, more permanent and weighty than any pang or thrill or happiness they've ever felt before. They'd have no way of comprehending that his joy isn't a switch we can turn on, an automatic setting we can dial up without having said two words to him the last three weeks. His joy is not a Tootsie Roll jar passed around for anybody who wants a piece.

Instead it's something much sweeter, much richer, much more fulfilling. That's because the Spirit's done the hard work to make us ready to receive his pure satisfaction.

> READ
> 1 THESSALONIANS
> 1:5–10

JOYFUL, JOYFUL, WE ADORE THEE

Oh, I'm not saying for one minute that we should ever—*ever!*—apologize about the joy we feel from our relationship with the Spirit. We should embrace it, celebrate it, fling ourselves back into it the way they used to do the old Nestea plunge on television.

But before we can truly experience his joy, we must let him do in us those hard-fought things we've been talking about up to now.

We must give him room to convict us of our sins—helping us see them for the filthy pollutants they really are, repenting of them, letting him purge them out of our hearts like toxins flushed from our system. Sin is a joy eater. Makes you wonder why we love it so.

We must give him permission to guide our steps in whatever direction he desires—forfeiting our own autonomy, learning to realize that the paths we think up ourselves are fatally flawed by our own flesh, our own agendas, and our own shortsightedness.

We must let his Word become our daily diet of truth—believing what he says no matter how we happen to feel about it at the moment, no matter how many excuses we want to make for asking him to meet us halfway. There's no joy to be had by hanging on to our own opinions or by foregoing faith just to keep our friends happy.

But as a result of the Holy Spirit's hardworking traits, he lets us experience a joy you simply cannot find at the bottom of a Ben and Jerry's cup. It's a zest for life that only comes from being kept pure and led eternally.

READ
ACTS 13:48–52

SOMETHING FUN TO DO

Ask the seventy who were sent out by Jesus, commissioned to give people the heads-up that the Son of God was coming to their town. The joy they received from the Spirit as they made connections, met needs, and mingled with the crowds was a *hundred* times better than if he'd just handed it to them one day after lunch.

What they discovered at each village was the fact that real joy comes from being employed by the Spirit to perform his work. They felt it every time they brought a smile to a troubled face, every time they amazed even themselves by seeing a crippled girl healed or a demon scrammed at one word from their mouths. They knew God was doing something in them and *through* them that they could never do on their own.

So, no, the unbelievers don't get to have all the fun.

In fact, there's nothing more exhilarating, more electrifying, than being a power tool in the hand of God. And we have the joyful option of being one every day. Sound like fun to you?

READ
ROMANS 15:13

DIG IN

Some really neat things are happening in Luke 10, and the Spirit makes sure we experience them all.

"THE SEVENTY RETURNED WITH JOY" (V. 17). Jesus had sent them out to minister in his name, and his Spirit working through them had filled them with joy. Talk about how that feels.

....
....
....
....
....

"IN THAT SAME HOUR HE REJOICED IN THE HOLY SPIRIT" (V. 21). Even Jesus himself depended on the Spirit for his joy supply. Why is everything else bland and empty by comparison?

....
....
....
....
....

"THE EYES THAT SEE THE THINGS YOU SEE ARE BLESSED!" (V. 23). What have you seen lately through your spiritual eyes that has blessed you with joy and gladness and encouragement?

....
....
....
....
....

EXPERIENCING GOD THE SPIRIT OVER AND OVER AGAIN

1. THE SPIRIT IS A GIFT FROM THE FATHER.
2. THE SPIRIT EXPOSES AND CONVICTS US OF SIN.
3. THE SPIRIT RENEWS, RESTORES, AND REFRESHES.
4. THE SPIRIT SETS US APART FOR SPECIAL SERVICE.
5. THE SPIRIT INDWELLS THOSE WHO BELONG TO HIM.
6. THE SPIRIT GIVES US GUIDANCE AND DIRECTION.
7. THE SPIRIT EMPOWERS AND EMBOLDENS US.
8. THE SPIRIT GIVES US INSIGHT INTO GOD'S PLANS.
9. THE SPIRIT CAN BE GRIEVED AND REBELLED AGAINST.
10. THE SPIRIT INSTRUCTS US IN THE WILL OF GOD.
11. THE SPIRIT MOVES AND REPOSITIONS HIS PEOPLE.
12. THE SPIRIT UNITES THE CHURCH IN MISSION.
13. THE SPIRIT FILLS US WITH JOY AND WORSHIP.
    "The kingdom of God is not eating and drinking" or going to movies, or shopping for sweaters, or listening to jazz music. Those things are fine and fun, but they cash out their full payment to you almost immediately. Once you've used them up, they're pretty much out of gas. "The kingdom of God," though, is "righteousness, peace, and joy in the Holy Spirit" (ROM. 14:17) —gifts that never stop giving.
14. THE SPIRIT ENDURES WITH US TO THE END.

PRAY ABOUT

- Anything that's keeping you from having Holy Spirit joy.
- An eagerness to tell others what serving him does for you.
- Those who need joy but don't know where to look for it.

FOURTEEN

TILL THE
BETTER END

I was sowing some grass seed in our backyard the other day. And granted, I'm no expert on anything agricultural. So I'm fully prepared to be told that this is one documented example where there really is such a thing as a stupid question.

But I'll ask it anyway: *Why doesn't the grass seed grow in the bag?*

What is it about tossing it on the ground, mixing it up with a little loose dirt, and sprinkling water on top of it that makes grass seed know it's time to start sprouting? I mean, what's it been waiting for all this time? Two months from now, when I go out to get that same seed bag from the shed, needing to broadcast some more handfuls into a few bare patches, why won't I find a bunch of thin, tender blades of Kentucky fescue in there instead?

(I sure hope none of my old schoolteachers are reading this.)

Let's just say that what happens inside that bag is nothing compared to what God does with those seeds later on. And let's likewise be glad that his Spirit will always be here with us while we wait for our day in the sun.

Dear Holy Spirit, I can't imagine making it through one day without your help. Thank you for assuring us that you'll always be here with us.

For I consider that the sufferings of this present time are not worth comparing with the glory that is going to be revealed in us. For the *creation eagerly waits with anticipation for God's sons to be revealed.* For the creation was subjected to futility—not willingly, but because of Him who subjected it—in the hope that the creation itself will also be set free from the bondage of corruption into the glorious freedom of God's children. For we know that the whole creation has been groaning together with labor pains until now. And not only that, but we ourselves who have the Spirit as the firstfruits— *we also groan within ourselves, eagerly waiting for adoption,* the redemption of our bodies. Now in this hope we were saved, yet hope that is seen is not hope, because who hopes for what he sees? But if we hope for what we do not see, we eagerly wait for it with patience.

In the same way *the Spirit also joins to help in our weakness,* because we do not know what to pray for as we should, but the Spirit Himself intercedes for us with unspoken groanings. And He who searches the hearts knows the Spirit's mind-set, because He intercedes for the saints according to the will of God.

Seems like this earth walk could have been plenty beneficial for us without having to be so witheringly hard at times. I'd fear that I was overexaggerating about this a little, if not for the fact that the Bible comes right out and admits (see ROM. 8) that "the whole creation has been groaning," struggling, suffering, fighting to get through this long interlude between now and forever.

So it's not just a few of us who sometimes feel this way.

Even when we take our life with Christ seriously, it can still be a tall order to stay submitted and keep our senses sharp. There are some days when being spiritual feels nearly impossible, if not at least highly inconvenient. We don't always approach each sunrise with both windows thrown open to the wind.

But you know what? *Life isn't supposed to be easy.* Learning to walk in obedience to the Spirit is an ongoing process that he patiently guides us through, constantly teaching us new things, whether from our own mistakes or from the encouragement of actually seeing his truths break out on us in the middle of the afternoon.

So without saying that we should ever treat lightly any of our sins against the Spirit, we need to remember that he is always here to pick us up and keep us going. Though we have no reason for putting any confidence in ourselves, we have every reason to rest in his continual presence. Now and forever.

> READ
> 2 CORINTHIANS 5:1–5

CAN'T WAIT TO MEET YOU

In fact, we have more than a human lifetime to be led by his loving direction. In eternity, even though we'll finally be able to follow him perfectly—(Won't *that* be wonderful!)—it will still be the Spirit we're following, the sweet presence of God.

That's why it's probably a little curious that when we think about heaven, we often imagine what it'll be like to see the Father in all his glory. We wonder what Jesus will look like when we finally lay eyes on him. But I don't think I've ever heard anybody say how eagerly they're looking forward to meeting the Holy Spirit.

Perhaps we should.

He's like a pen pal we've developed a relationship with in letters, like a radio announcer we've heard delivering the news for years on our favorite station. We've gotten to know his voice. We could pick it out even if we were someplace where we weren't expecting to hear it. We know his inflections, his sense of humor, the phrases he often repeats.

Seeing him one day with our own eyes would really be special.

So for now we keep listening, loving him for the tingle we feel in every skin cell when his presence is indescribably real. We keep waiting, knowing that this same voice that resonates within us is even now interceding for us before the Father. We keep believing, assured that the redemptive work of Christ he's continually renewing in our hearts will keep working its way through our actions and attitudes.

R E A D
GALATIANS 5:4–6

We keep on because so does he.

YOU MEAN THERE'S MORE?

The concept the Scriptures use most often in helping explain the role of the Holy Spirit in our lives is that of a "down payment." More than once Paul returns to this idea, helping us see that the portion of God's presence we get to experience each day while we're padding around here in shoe leather is only a percentage of his visible glory.

The Spirit is but a taste, a mere glimpse of the greatness we'll one day get to see and feel and perceive.

And though we're already kept safe and secure in Christ even by the "down payment" part of his Spirit, we are readily assured that the final summing up of our salvation—our ultimate rescue from judgment and death—is awaiting us one for-sure day in the future. Until then, we are "sealed with the promised Holy Spirit" (EPH. 1:13), surrounded by his protection, engulfed in his purpose, infused with his power.

If it seems hard to realize it on some days, that's OK. Just try to remember that the mortgage on your heavenly mansion is already paid. And the "down payment" alone is more than enough to keep us afloat till we get there.

R E A D
EPHESIANS 1:13–14

DIG IN

This chunk of ROMANS 8 moves from Genesis to Revelation but slows down enough to pick us up along the way.

"CREATION EAGERLY WAITS WITH ANTICIPATION FOR GOD'S SONS TO BE REVEALED" (V. 19). What a strange statement. How do you think the "new creation" will be different from this one?

....

....

....

"WE ALSO GROAN WITHIN OURSELVES, EAGERLY WAITING FOR ADOPTION" (V. 23). In what ways do you personally experience this gnawing, not-quite-there unsettledness in your spirit?

....

....

....

....

....

"THE SPIRIT ALSO JOINS TO HELP US IN OUR WEAKNESS" (V. 26). This assistance is something we can count on until the day we die. Think about how he's bringing his help to you today.

....

....

....

....

....

Experiencing God the Spirit Over and Over Again

1. The Spriit is a gift from the Father.
2. The Spirit exposes and convicts us of sin.
3. The Spirit renews, restores, and refreshes.
4. The Spirit sets us apart for special service.
5. The Spirit indwells those who belong to him.
6. The Spirit gives us guidance and direction.
7. The Spirit empowers and emboldens us.
8. The Spirit gives us insight into God's plan.
9. The Spirit can be grieved and rebelled against.
10. The Spirit instructs us in the will of God.
11. The Spirit moves and repositions his people.
12. The Spirit unites the church in mission.
13. The Spirit fills us with joy and worship.
14. The Spirit endures with us to the end.

All the wonderful blessings we receive at the hand of the Holy Spirit wouldn't add up to much if they came with an expiration date. But even on days when we're tired of trying, when we're impatient with God and ourselves, remember that the "Spirit of the Lord" is never impatient (Mic. 2:7). He just keeps going on and keeps us going on in the process.

Pray About

- Whatever it takes to walk more intimately with the Spirit.
- How to live out your trust in his leading and care each day.
- Keeping your spirit eternally minded, even on Tuesdays.

ALSO AVAILABLE:

If you enjoyed using this book, try others in the series.

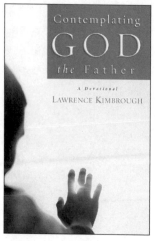

Contemplating God the Father
ISBN: 0-8054-4083-6

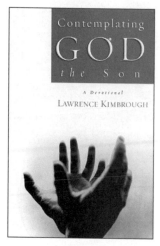

Contemplating God the Son
ISBN: 0-8054-4084-4

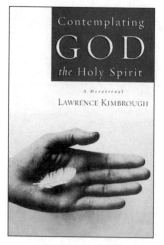

Contemplating God the Holy Spirit
ISBN: 0-8054-4085-2

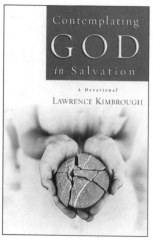

Contemplating God in Salvation
ISBN: 0-8054-4086-0

Find them in stores or at www.broadmanholman.com